SEX, SPEECH, SELFIES, AND GETTING SMASHED

SEX, SPEECH, SELFIES, AND GETTING SMASHED

Critical Legal Issues for College Students

C. L. Lindsay III

cognella®
SAN DIEGO

Bassim Hamadeh, CEO and Publisher
Amy Smith, Senior Project Editor
Rachel Kahn, Production Editor
Emely Villavicencio, Senior Graphic Designer
Kylie Bartolome, Licensing Associate
Natalie Piccotti, Director of Marketing
Kassie Graves, Senior Vice President, Editorial
Jamie Giganti, Director of Academic Publishing

320 South Cedros Ave., Ste. 400, Solana Beach, CA 92075

Brief Contents

Detailed Contents

PART II Sex   41

CHAPTER 3

Sex Crimes: Streaking to Stalking   42

CHAPTER 4

Title IX and Sexual Assault   56

PART IV Drugs, Alcohol, and Parties   111

Every effort has been made to ensure that this text contains the most up-to-date, accurate, and effective information available but laws and regulations change frequently and are subject to differing interpretations. Because it is written with the broadest possible audience in mind, this book addresses general legal issues only. The information and advice given may or may not be appropriate to a specific situation. Nothing contained in the book is legal advice and should not be relied on as such. It is not intended to create, and does not create, a lawyer-client relationship. It is not a substitute for legal counsel in the relevant jurisdiction.

Acknowledgments

I've spent the last 20 years giving lectures on campuses across the country. Ostensibly I'm there to do the teaching. But each visit is a learning experience for me too. The questions and problems we work through keep me sharp and help me stay informed about pressing issues. But most of all, those visits continually remind me that the education community is filled with amazing, caring, and dedicated people. Thank you to every school that's hosted me over the last two decades. I'm proud to work among you.

Beyond that, there have been a handful of individuals at schools and other institutions who have been particularly supportive and helpful over the years. They include

Nick Luchko at DeSales University;
Alicia Dunphy-Culp at Villanova University;
Lora Pace at Morehead State University;
Amanda Lopez and Corey Headley at South Dakota School of Mines & Technology;
Heidi Goettl at Concordia University, St. Paul;
Lara Cummings and John Klasen at Glenbrook South High School;
Michelle Ahlquist, Cindy Haarstad, and Kelly Hughes at Alexandria Technical & Community College;
Dave Zamansky at Colby-Sawyer College;
Lynn Rasch and Mike Squires at Culver Academies;
Lisa Bartram at University of the Cumberlands;
Sarah Rine and Michael Kennedy at UMass Lowell;
Chris Pearson and Susie Paunan at New Trier High School;
Susan Liebau, Alan Turnquist, and Steve Jones at Michigan Technological University;
Dave Blandford at Alma College;
Kyle Croy at Southwestern Oregon Community College;
Tia Steele at Augustana College;
Cynthia Hutchinson at Rocky Mountain College;
Brandi Storgaard at the South Dakota Network Against Family Violence and Sexual Assault;

> Callie Clark at Clarke University;
> Zac Pace;
> Emily Louden;
> Randy Flowers;
> Jessica Berkey-Barnes at Furman University;
> Kevin Carmody at Grand Valley State University;
> Seth Vander Tuig at Kirkwood Community College;
> Randall Paterson at the University of Connecticut;
> Jess Flynn and Jennie Hemingway at Illinois College;
> John Seckel at St. Norbert College;
> Megan Reiffenberger at Lake Area Technical College; and
> Chelsea Reisch at Southeast Technical College.

Thanks also to Kassie Graves, Amy Smith, Rachel Kahn, Emely Villavicencio, Tiffany Mok, and everyone else at Cognella for their hard work on this book.

And finally, a special thanks to everyone at Bass Schuler Entertainment—Scott and Mia Bass, Chris Schuler, Sue Boxrud, Rachel Wolfson, Christina Bravo, Amanda Hranicka, Sharon Sellers, Carolyn Riehl-Mitchell, Bec Hunter, Drew Korb, and Kristine Jurcevic-Edgworth—who worked tirelessly for the past 20 years booking lectures, coordinating with schools, and completing untold amounts of paperwork on my behalf. Without you, I don't know where I'd be.

Introduction

My job in this book is to teach you how to avoid trouble and keep you safe. Because of that, I mostly focus on the darker side of the justice and disciplinary systems. These pages are filled with horror stories detailing times when the law wasn't followed or didn't provide adequate protection.

That information is important. But I don't want you to finish this text thinking that the law trades only in misery. Because it can also be a powerful tool for good. You can use it to stand up for your rights, to protect the things you care about, and even to make the world a better place. Title IX, covered in chapter 4, is a perfect example. There, it's mostly discussed in relation to sexual assaults. It's the statute that gives schools the authority to punish offenders. But Title IX is so much more. It radically transformed higher education for the better. It's touched every corner of campus life and moved gender equality forward in sports, admissions, hiring, promotions and more.

Please don't forget this upside of the legal system as you read. Our laws, though far from perfect, are one of the things that make this country extraordinary. And if they're used correctly, they have the power to make America a better, safer, and fairer place.

WHAT IS A LAW?

There's much more to a statute than the actual words on the page. Examining the text is, of course, the first step in understanding it. But that static language is only a fraction of the story. To truly know how a law works, you have to examine its entire judicial history.

Consider the First Amendment. It's spawned thousands of lawsuits, each one further delineating its application in the real world. You'll read a lot about this in chapter 1, which is basically a discussion of the difference between the First Amendment as written and its enforcement. The pertinent part, "Congress shall make no law ... abridging the freedom of speech,"[1] is simple and definitive. But the courts have added dozens of exceptions, qualifications, and refinements to that plain statement over the last 200 years: You can't incite violence[2] or threaten people,[3] you can't make noise late at night,[4] you can't possess child pornography,[5] and so on.

This applies to mundane rules too. In chapter 7 you'll learn about underage drinking statutes. You'll quickly see that seemingly simple concepts can also be hard to pin down. Take underage possession, for example. Most state laws basically say, "No one under 21 years of age may possess alcohol." But what does that mean? If a teen is driving a car with a case of beer locked in the trunk, does that count? Or does the alcohol actually have to be in their hands? What if they're working as a server in a bar? What about cough medicine or vanilla extract? Both can contain alcohol. Do those trace amounts count?

This is because laws, as written, are finite. Situations are nearly infinite. In between is a complicated and never-ending dance performed by the judicial system that's an attempt to bridge the gap. This is critical to keep in mind as you learn about the law on campus. Whenever possible, I'll point out bright line rules. But more often, the best I'll be able to do is explain the most recent step in this process. I'll offer guidelines and a brief accounting of the history of the law being discussed. Applying a statute to a specific situation, then, will require extrapolation on your part.

One more point about laws: Reading them can seem intimidating. That's partly because lawyers like to perpetuate the myth that they're the only ones who can decode legalese. I assure you that's not true. There are no special skills needed. You'll need to comb through the language deliberately and carefully think about what every clause and punctuation mark means. But if you go slowly, especially at first, you should have no trouble at all.

PUBLIC VERSUS PRIVATE SCHOOLS

Many of the privileges we closely associate with being American are derived from the Constitution, more specifically the Bill of Rights. Those first 10 Amendments are the basis for the definitive liberties we enjoy as U.S. citizens.

Two of those, the First and Fourth Amendments, figure largely in this book and, in turn, may affect your time at college. The First Amendment is the subject of the opening section, free speech. The Fourth Amendment, which protects citizens from unreasonable search and seizure, is examined in chapters 6 and 8. As you'll learn, these laws aren't absolute. There are many caveats. But the most critical for you, as a college student, has to do with the kind of school you attend.

The Bill of Rights only applies to government entities, also called "state actors." Public colleges and universities are part of the government. Private colleges, of course, aren't. Public schools, therefore, are required to grant you the freedoms delineated in the Bill of Rights. Not so for private institutions. For the most part, they can do what they want.

Throughout the book, when the public-private school distinction matters, I'll point it out and explain how it applies to that specific situation. But it's important for you to know at the outset that the type of college you go to can drastically affect your rights.

ON-CAMPUS DISCIPLINE VERSUS THE COURTS

Court cases and disciplinary hearings are distinctly different entities. Still, students confuse the two. Or, more often, they subconsciously overlay what they think they know about lawsuits onto the campus disciplinary system. That's a big mistake because the accused have far fewer rights on campus than they do in court.

This is yet another area where the public-private school difference is critical. Public colleges are bound by the due process clause of the Fifth Amendment. That means they can't deprive anyone of "life, liberty, or property" without a fair hearing. Since schools don't execute or imprison their students, the "life" and "liberty" parts don't apply. However, you do have a property interest in your education and your reputation. Being expelled could do serious damage to both.

Therefore, when the charges are serious, public schools have to take steps to ensure the hearings are fair. But that doesn't amount to much in the way of tangible requirements. They have to give the accused notice of the charges against them, inform them of the evidence that implicates them, and give them a chance to present their side of the story.[6] That's all. Private schools, technically, don't even have to provide those basic tenets of due process. They're not state actors. The Fifth doesn't apply.

That's drastically different than what's required in court. In an actual judicial proceeding there are myriad complex rules in place to ensure impartiality. None of them apply to disciplinary systems. Schools, be they public or private, don't have to follow the rules of evidence or read you your rights. They don't have to give you an opportunity to cross examine witnesses or allow an attorney to represent you. You don't even have a right to appeal the decision if the hearing goes against you. Forget everything you learned from *Law & Order* reruns. None of that knowledge is going to help you in an on-campus hearing.

YOUR SCHOOL'S RULES

As you've probably begun to realize, your rights at school rest on a complex and nebulous foundation. Higher education law involves a mix of state laws, court decisions, federal statutes, and governmental guidance that often overlap and are sometimes in direct conflict. Even lawyers can have trouble determining which set of rules is controlling.

There is, however, one source of campus "law" that's iron clad—your college's own policies. The publication of those rules creates a contract between you and the university. This is the case at both public and private institutions. Every school has to follow its own rules. If, for example, the academic dishonesty policy says accused students will get a hearing, then the school must provide that hearing. Or, if your housing agreement states that rooms can't be searched without permission, resident advisors have to stay out unless you tell them they can come in.

Therefore, your school's policies are, far and away, the most important set of rules you'll encounter while attending college. They directly define your relationship with the university and govern your entire life—academic, residential, and to some extent social.

They're incredibly easy to find. I guarantee that they're included, in their entirety, on the school's website. A simple search on the homepage or in the student portal will bring them up. Still, most students haven't even taken a passing glance at them. Don't be one of the uninformed. Get familiar with your school's policies and regulations. And when a problem arises on campus, they should be the first rules you consult, because until you graduate, they're as important as the U.S. Constitution.

NOTES

1   U.S. Constitution, First Amendment.
2   Chaplinsky v. State of New Hampshire, 315 U.S. 568 (1942).

3   Virginia v. Black et al., 538 U.S. 343 (2003).
4   Ward v. Rock Against Racism, 491 U.S. 781 (1989).
5   Feiner v. New York, 340 U.S. 315 (1951).
6   Goss v. Lopez, 419 U.S. 565 (1975).

PART I

SPEECH

Some questions have clear answers. Like middle school math problems, there's a definitive truth. The area of a triangle is half of the base times the height. The square root of 100 can't be anything other than 10. A lot of what you studied in high school was probably presented this way—details to recite, facts and figures you had to know.

That's not how the law operates. Often, the deeper you get into an issue the more questions you'll have. Broad legal concepts, like those contained in the Bill of Rights, are particularly hard to pin down. This is especially true with the First Amendment. There are guidelines and principles, but the fact patterns rarely fall neatly into one category or another. Whether or not something is protected speech is often a judgment call. And a small detail about a case can change the ruling. Beyond that, it's an area where the courts have been maddeningly inconsistent.

Reading this section, then, won't give you the ability to find yes or no answers to First Amendment issues. That's not possible. Instead, you should finish with a working free speech vocabulary that will help you better understand the questions themselves. When an issue arises at your school, you'll be able to see the rough contours and the complexity of the problem. Don't worry if it feels like the ground is shifting under you a little as you go through this section. You should get to the end of chapter 2 realizing that "probably yes" or "maybe no" is often the most solid First Amendment footing you can hope for.

I want to make one more point before we get to the specifics of free speech law. We tend to focus mainly on what the First Amendment protects: the right to express ourselves. Please, don't lose sight of the other side of the equation—listening. Speech doesn't matter at all if no one hears it. It's your duty, as a student, as an American, and as a human to seriously consider what others say. Even if you're sure someone's dead wrong, at least let them explain themselves before you shut them down.

I think you should go further. You're at college. You physically inhabit a marketplace of ideas. Take advantage. Seek out viewpoints other than your own. Try to really understand what motivates those who oppose what you hold most dear. For me, the First Amendment is more about hearing what others have to say than screaming what you're certain is true. It exists to ensure that, as a nation, we keep communicating with each other about important issues.

FREE SPEECH ON CAMPUS

PIAROWSKI'S SHOCKING STAINED GLASS

The art department at Prairie State College (a community college just south of Chicago) opened their annual faculty exhibition in the spring of 1980. Each professor chose their own works to display. Albert Piarowski, the department chair, selected eight stained glass windows for the exhibit. They were mounted in an alcove just off "the mall"—the busiest space in the main building on campus. The gallery wasn't walled off. The pieces could be easily seen by anyone who walked by.[1]

Piarowski's windows weren't exactly Louis Comfort Tiffany. This is how the court described them:

> Five were abstract; three were representational and became the focus of controversy. One depicts the naked rump of a brown woman, and sticking out from (or into) it a white cylinder that resembles a finger but on careful inspection is seen to be a jet of gas. Another window shows a brown woman from the back, standing, naked except for stockings, and apparently masturbating. In the third window another brown woman, also naked except for stockings and also seen from the rear, is crouching in a posture of veneration before a robed white male whose most prominent feature is a grotesquely outsized phallus (erect penis) that the woman is embracing.[2]

A number of students, some cleaning staff, and a local reverend complained to the university about the art (although it's not clear if the reverend actually saw the panels or just heard about them).[3] The university asked Piarowski to move his works to a less conspicuous space—a gallery upstairs. He refused. Ten days after they were hung, the university took the panels down.[4]

Piarowski sued the school for violating his First Amendment rights. He lost. In its ruling the court said:

> When we consider that the expression in this case was not political, that it was regulated rather than suppressed, that the plaintiff is not only a faculty member but an administrator, that good alternative sites may have been available to him, and that in short he is claiming a First Amendment right to exhibit sexually explicit and racially offensive art work in what amounts to the busiest corridor in a college that employs him in a responsible administrative as well as academic position, we are driven to conclude that the defendants did not infringe the plaintiff's First Amendment rights merely by ordering him to move the art to another room in the same building.[5]

Do you agree? Do you think the school should have taken the art down? What if this happened on your campus? Imagine one of your classmates is a photographer. His subjects are edgy. He's like a modern-day Robert Mapplethorpe. The photos feature graphic nudity, sexuality, and bondage. Which of the following options do you think is fair?

→ He's a student. His art has value. It should be hung on the walls in the student union where everyone will see it.
→ He should be able to show his work. But it should be in a designated gallery, not the busiest room on campus.
→ His work could offend or trigger people. It should be in a gallery with a door. And there should be a sign or a docent outside to warn visitors about the graphic nature of the images.
→ He can make the art. But the school shouldn't allow him to display it on campus. It's too provocative.
→ Art like that has no place at a college. He should make it elsewhere if he wants.

Personally, I land on number 2. But there are solid arguments to be made for other options. And that's the point: With any First Amendment issue there are always two sides, often more. Each party has rights and interests that need to be considered. Piarowski had a right to create his art. The school had a need to protect its image. Students should be able walk through campus without being confronted by triggering images. Compromises need to be made. This is especially true at a college. A school should allow free expression, but it also has a duty to maintain an environment free from harassment and discrimination.

FREE SPEECH BASICS

State Actors Only

This is the First Amendment to the U.S. Constitution. It applies to the federal government, and through the 14th Amendment, extends to state governments:

> Congress shall make no law respecting an establishment of religion, or prohibiting the free exercise thereof; or abridging the freedom of speech, or of the press; or the right of the people peaceably to assemble, and to petition the Government for a redress of grievances.[6]

It's the legal source of your right to free speech. Actually, the phrase "free expression" is more accurate. The First Amendment protects far more than words. It covers art, music, fashion choices (e.g., black armbands), and actions (e.g., burning the flag). Almost any way you can express yourself is "speech" under the First Amendment.

As is discussed elsewhere, the entire Bill of Rights only applies to the government (also called state actors). Public schools, therefore, have to adhere to the First Amendment. Private colleges don't. The exception to this rule is California. There, a state statute called the Leonard Law extends First Amendment protections to students at private colleges and universities. Still, private California schools that are "controlled by a religious organization" don't have to allow speech that's inconsistent "with the religious tenets of the organization."[7]

This public/private distinction is incredibly important. And it will become even more critical once you graduate. Most college students attend public schools—almost 78% of undergrads are enrolled at public institutions[8] and are, therefore, protected by the First Amendment. In the real world, the ratio flips. In 2021 only 14% of the workforce was employed directly by federal and state governments.[9] Chances are, after you graduate the people who sign your paycheck will be able to fire you if they don't like what you say.

Consider the case of Bart Hubbuch. He'd been a sports writer, covering the NFL, at the *New York Post* for 10 years. On the day of Trump's inauguration he tweeted "12/7/41. 9/11/01. 1/20/17."—comparing the beginning of Trump's presidency to Pearl Harbor and the 9/11 attacks.

The *Post*, a private company owned by Rupert Murdoch, fired him.[10] Hubbuch tweeted on his own time, from a personal Twitter account, about a subject of national concern that had nothing to do with his job. But First Amendment constraints don't apply to private employers.

And, even if you do work for the government, there are limits. If your speech affects your ability to do your job or negatively impacts your employer, they can terminate you regardless of your First Amendment rights. A 2000 case concerning a San Diego policeman illustrates this well. The department fired one of their officers for selling explicit videos on eBay. In the films he would strip out of a police uniform (not an official one, a costume) and perform sex acts. The department said his videos violated the force's moral conduct policy and, further, that performing in pornography was conduct unbecoming an officer. The officer sued, arguing that the dismissal violated his First Amendment right to express himself. The Supreme Court upheld his firing. They said his side gig making cop erotica was "detrimental to the mission and functions" of his employer.[11]

Exceptions to Free Speech

The right to express yourself under the First Amendment isn't absolute. The government can regulate speech in a few ways. These fall into two broad categories: **content-based restrictions** and **time, place, and manner restrictions**. Content-based restrictions are exactly what they sound like—types of expression that aren't allowed due to their meaning. You have no right to express yourself in these ways. If you do, a public school could discipline you, a public employer could fire you, or the justice system could punish you. The exceptions based on content are incredibly limited.

Time, place, and manner restrictions don't have anything to do with what's being communicated. They're about how the speech is being broadcast. State actors can make reasonable rules about where, how loudly, or when someone can express themselves. You're not allowed to scream about voting rights outside a hospital. The actual words might be protected by the First Amendment, but you can't disturb patients who are trying to sleep and heal. Similarly, if you're running for office, you have a right to make political speeches. But you can't set up a podium in the middle of a four-lane highway to detail your campaign promises. That's unsafe. And it would cause horrible traffic jams.

We'll look at these two categories of exceptions to the First Amendments protections in detail.

Content-Based Restrictions

Speech That Breaks the Law

If the speech is itself a violation of the law, the First Amendment offers no protection. For example, it's illegal to solicit someone else to commit a crime. Similarly, lying under oath in a court is the crime of perjury. The First Amendment also doesn't protect blackmailers. Libel and slander would also fall into this category—although defamation suits are brought by private citizens, not the government.

Fighting Words

This is one of the more famous free speech exceptions. Despite its notoriety, the fighting words exception is actually very narrow. It was first laid out by the Supreme Court in *Chaplinsky v. New Hampshire*, a case decided in 1942. Chaplinsky, a Jehovah's Witness, was handing out pamphlets and making a fiery speech on the sidewalk near a busy intersection. He denounced organized religion as a "racket." By today's standards that may seem tame, but apparently in the 1940s that was enough to rile up a crowd of locals. A "disturbance" ensued, and a traffic cop detained Chaplinsky. On their way to the police station for booking, the two encountered the town marshal. Chaplinsky called the marshal a "God damned racketeer" and a "damned fascist."

For those two insults, Chaplinsky was convicted of violating a local law that prohibited addressing any "offensive, derisive, or annoying word to any other person who is lawfully in any street or other public place, nor call him by any offensive or derisive name."

He appealed, arguing his First Amendment rights were violated. The Supreme Court upheld his conviction. Calling someone a "fascist" and a "racketeer," they said, was so offensive and inflammatory it invited physical retaliation (i.e., they were "fighting words"). Again, this was 80 years ago. Sensibilities have changed. I can't imagine that any current court would consider calling someone a racketeer fighting words. Still, the Chaplinsky's case was the genesis of today's fighting words doctrine.[12]

Over the years a three-prong test has been developed to determine if speech amounts to fighting words:

1. The speech has to be directed at a specific individual.
2. It has to be so offensive that it will cause an immediate violent response—this immediacy is key.

3.   The speech can't have any redeemable expressive value (e.g., political commentary or artistic merit).[13]

Think carefully about what each requirement means. You'll start to get a sense of how rarely speech that's offensive qualifies as "fighting words." Some legal scholars actually think that the fighting words doctrine has been so reigned in, it's effectively dead.

Also, this is an area in which courts have been horribly inconsistent. Similar cases come out differently depending on which judge decided it. In 2003 the 3rd Circuit found that calling a police officer a "son of a bitch" was protected speech.[14] But in 1999 the Maine Supreme Court found that calling a cop a "fucking asshole" and spitting at him constituted fighting words.[15] Maybe the spitting put him over the edge. At any rate, this is an exception that's hard to pin down.

Incitement to Imminent Lawless Action

Closely related to the fighting words exception is the doctrine laid out in *Brandenburg v. Ohio*—speech that incites immediate lawless action.

In 1964 Clarence Brandenburg held a Ku Klux Klan rally at a farm near Cincinnati, Ohio. He invited a local TV station to come and film the event. *Rally* is actually too big of a word for what happened. There were only a dozen participants. They burned a cross, and Brandenburg made a speech for the cameras where he said, "We're not a revengent organization, but if our president, our congress, our Supreme Court, continues to suppress the white, Caucasian race, it's possible that there might have to be some revengeance taken."[16]

For uttering those words (including the made-up ones) Brandenburg was convicted under Ohio's Criminal Syndicalism Law, which made it illegal to "advocate … the duty, necessity, or propriety of crime, sabotage, or unlawful methods of terrorism as a means of accomplishing industrial or political reform."[17]

The Supreme Court overturned his conviction. The court said speech could only be punished when it was "directed to inciting or producing imminent lawless action and is likely to incite or produce such action."[18] As in the fighting words exception the danger had to be immediate to be outside First Amendment protection. Here there were just 12 racists out in a field. There was no real possibility of imminent unlawful actions. Sure, Brandenburg's speech hinted at "revengeance." But it was theoretical and in the distant future.

Clarence Brandenburg (left) posing for a picture after his arrest in 1948.

True Threats

Threats aren't protected by the First Amendment either. But they must be "true threats," meaning they have to communicate a real intent to harm directed at a specific person. The Supreme Court discussed this in *Virginia v. Black* (2003).[19] The case involved two separate cross burnings. One was at a Ku Klux Klan rally held on private property with the permission of the owner. In the other, three men stuck a burning cross in the front yard of an African American family in the middle of the night. At the time Virginia had a statute that outlawed cross burning:

> It shall be unlawful for any person or persons, with the intent of intimidating any person or group of persons, to burn, or cause to be burned, a cross on the property of another, a highway or other public place.[20]

The Supreme Court's opinion hinged on the intent requirement. They found that the burning of the cross out in the field was constitutionally protected speech because it was merely an expression of an ideology and not directed at a specific person. The lawn cross burning was different, they said. It wasn't protected speech. It was aimed at a specific family with the intent to intimidate. Therefore, that incident was a "true threat."[21]

Obscenity

Obscene materials aren't protected by the First Amendment. The famous line "I'll know it when I see it"[22] isn't the actual legal standard for determining what is and isn't obscene. That was written by Justice Potter Stewart in an opinion that's long since been overturned. The actual standard was laid out in *Miller v. California* (1973).[23] Something is "obscene"

1. if the average person applying contemporary community standards would think that the work, taken as a whole, appeals to a prurient (meaning dirty) interest;
2. if the work depicts or describes sex or excretory functions in a patently offensive way; and
3. if the work, taken as a whole, lacks serious literary, artistic, political, or scientific value.[24]

Think back to Piarowski's stained glass panels. They're clearly not obscene under the Miller test. As the court said, they "are not very realistic; seem not intended to arouse, titillate, or disgust and are not wholly devoid of artistic merit, or at least artistic intention."[25]

The vast majority of pornography wouldn't be obscene under this test either—although the "contemporary community standards" part is problematic. Some communities are more prudish than others. What's perfectly acceptable in San Francisco or New York may be seen as inexcusably dirty in a small midwestern town.

Child Pornography

And finally, child pornography is never protected by the First Amendment. In a 1982 case, *New York v. Ferber*, the Supreme Court held that child pornography can be banned without being deemed "obscene" under the *Miller* test. Among other things, the court said that the government had a compelling interest in protecting children from sexual abuse and, further, that child pornography had no artistic value. Therefore, it was within the states' rights to ban it entirely.[26]

Time, Place, and Manner Restrictions

As the Supreme Court stated in *Healy v. James*, "activities need not be tolerated where they infringe reasonable campus rules, interrupt classes, or substantially interfere with the opportunity of other students to obtain an education."[27] The government and your school can enforce time, place, and manner restrictions on speech. The simplest example of this kind of rule is a noise ordinance. Your town can certainly stop you from making a racket in the middle of the night even if what you're saying is protected speech.

Noise was at the center of one of the most important Supreme Court cases regarding time, place, and manner restrictions—*Ward v. Rock Against Racism* (1989).[28] The organizers of a concert, Rock Against Racism (RAR), rented the Naumberg Bandshell in New York City's Central Park. There had been a long history of noise problems there. To ensure events didn't disturb those nearby, the city required the use

FIGURE 1.2   The Naumberg Bandshell in Central Park.

of municipal sound equipment and a city-appointed technician who could ensure that the noise levels stayed in check.[29]

The RAR organizers sued, saying that the imposition of a city engineer and equipment violated their First Amendment right to express themselves. They lost. In the opinion the court laid out a three-point test (courts love three-point tests) to determine if a time, place, and manner restriction violated the First Amendment. For a regulation to be valid, they said it must

1. be content neutral;
2. be narrowly tailored to serve a significant governmental interest; and
3. leave plenty of alternative ways for the speaker to express themselves.[30]

You can see how this might play out on a college campus. A rule prohibiting events on the academic quad during class hours would pass the test. First, it's content neutral because it applies to everyone. Two, it's narrow and protects a legitimate interest of the school—a college needs to be able teach its students. Making sure they can hear their professors is necessary. Three, the rule applies to a distinct area on campus, leaving plenty of other times and places events could be held. Events after class hours would be allowed. And all of the other parts of the school's grounds could be used at any time of day.

In contrast, a rule that prohibited the distribution of Democratic election materials on campus but allowed Republican candidates to do whatever they wanted would violate the First because it's biased based on content. A policy that banned all political speech from an entire campus would also violate the First Amendment, because it doesn't meet parts 2 and 3 of the test. It's not "narrowly tailored" to accomplish a goal of the school, and it leaves no alternative means of expression open.

Free Speech Zones

In the 1980s and 1990s public schools across the country set aside distinct, and sometimes prohibitively small, spots on campus specifically for free expression.[31] That may sound like a nice idea, as if the college is actively supporting the First Amendment by saying "Here's a place to express yourself." But by designating one space for free expression the schools were essentially prohibiting free speech everywhere else on campus.

Apply the RAR test. Free speech zones are content neutral. But is limiting free speech to one spot on campus narrowly tailored to achieve a significant goal of the school? Of course not. Does it leave open ample other ways for students to get their messages out? Also no.

Even worse, schools often piled regulations on top of these zones. Students would have to register ahead of time to use them. Some zones had restrictive time limits. Consider the case of Kevin Shaw, a student at Pierce College, a public school in California. On November 2, 2016 Shaw and two non-students set up a table on campus. They put it outside along the main thoroughfare. They weren't blocking pedestrian access or disrupting campus activities in any way. They planned on passing out Spanish-language copies of the U.S. Constitution and wanted to engage students in discussions about the government.

A few minutes later a representative of the school arrived and told Shaw that the table wasn't allowed. They had set up outside the campus free speech zone and, even if it had been in the right spot, using the zone required preregistration. Shaw asked what would happen if he didn't register and was told that he'd be escorted off campus. Shaw immediately went to the administration building and filled out an application. When he asked for a copy of the completed form, the school said no.[32]

The college gave Shaw the runaround for the next month. The free speech zone policy wasn't on the school website nor in the student handbook. Shaw repeatedly asked administrators for a copy but was told no over and over. The school also refused to give him a copy of his own permit. Finally, in early December the administration relented and provided copies of both. During the same time period multiple large protests spontaneously erupted on campus (outside the free

    Kevin Shaw at Pierce College.

speech zone) in response to Trump's election. The school didn't interfere with any of those.[33]

Turns out, the free speech zone detailed in the policy was a 616 square foot rectangle. The Pierce campus is 426 acres. Free speech, therefore, was restricted to 0.03% of the school's land. And there was no mention of permits or registration in the policy. That was just an unwritten rule enforced by the administration.[34]

Shaw sued the school. He argued that the rules and regulations had a chilling effect of the freedom of expression and therefore violated the First Amendment. He also argued that the rules were applied inconsistently and unfairly, since some protests outside the zone were allowed but his table was prohibited.

The case settled out of court before it could be decided. As a part of the deal the school revoked the policy and paid $225,000 to cover Shaw's legal fees.[35] If it had gone to trial Shaw would almost certainly have won. When challenged in court, free speech zones are almost always found to be unconstitutional. Many states have even passed laws banning them altogether. At the time of writing 22 states had laws on the books prohibiting free speech zones on campuses.

TENSION WITH DISCRIMINATION STATUTES

Of course, the First Amendment isn't the only law that colleges have to follow. Title VI of the Civil Rights Act of 1964 states,

> No person in the United States shall, on the ground of race, color, or national origin, be excluded from participation in, be denied the benefits of, or be subjected to discrimination under any program or activity receiving Federal financial assistance.[36]

And Title IX of the Education Amendments of 1972 (which is discussed extensively in Chapter 4) says:

> No person in the United States shall, on the basis of sex, be excluded from participation in, be denied the benefits of, or be subjected to discrimination under any educational program or activity receiving Federal financial assistance.[37]

Together these two laws require that all colleges, public and private, maintain campuses that are free from race and gender harassment and discrimination. Those mandates include much more than fair admissions policies. They create an obligation on the part of schools to provide a welcoming environment for everyone to learn. In other words, schools can't allow a racist or sexist campus culture to exist.

Presumably then, schools need to prohibit racist and sexist speech in some instances. If you've been paying attention so far, that last sentence should make your head hurt a little. We just learned that public colleges can't prohibit expression based on its content unless it falls into one of the specific categories explained—illegal acts, fighting words, incitement, obscenity, or child pornography. And most racist and sexist speech doesn't fit into any of those exceptions.

How do public colleges reconcile these two competing sets of rules? It's an excellent question, and one without any clear answers.

Speech Codes

Universities have tried to maintain nondiscriminatory environments by enacting rules that prohibit offensive speech. The University of Wisconsin passed the first speech code in 1981.[38] By the mid 90s a majority of colleges had something similar in place. Many schools still have rules like these on the books. These regulations—while well intentioned—are often far too broad and vague. They suppress speech based on content and viewpoints. They do so in the name of Title VI and XI, but they also, often, run afoul of the First Amendment.

The first federal lawsuit to address speech codes was *Doe v. University of Michigan* (1989).[39] In the years leading up to that case there had been a rash of racist incidents on U of M's Ann Arbor campus. In January of 1987 someone distributed a flier calling for "open season" on African Americans—it referred to minorities as "saucer lips, porch monkeys, and jigaboos." In February a DJ on the campus radio station broadcasted racist jokes. Then, at a demonstration protesting the flier and the radio broadcast, a student displayed a KKK cloak in a nearby dorm window.[40]

In response, the Michigan administration instituted a speech policy that prohibited any "behavior, verbal or physical, that stigmatizes or victimizes an individual on the basis of race, ethnicity, religion, sex, sexual orientation, creed, national origin, ancestry, age, marital status, handicap or Vietnam-era veteran status."[41] They also published an interpretive guide that gave examples of sanctionable conduct. Included in that list were the following:

> "You exclude someone from a study group because that
> person is of a different race, sex, or ethnic origin than
> you are."
>
> "You comment in a derogatory way about a particular
> person or group's physical appearance or sexual orienta-
> tion, or their cultural origins, or religious beliefs."
>
> "Students in a residence hall have a floor party and
> invite everyone on their floor except one person because
> they think she might be a lesbian."[42]

A biopsychology graduate student sued the school. He argued that
the policy would prevent him from discussing controversial theories
in class because they could be perceived as racist or sexist.[43] A district
court held that the Michigan policy was, indeed, unconstitutional and
struck it down. In the opinion, they wrote that "while the Court is
sympathetic to the University's obligation to ensure equal educational
opportunities for all of its students, such efforts must not be at the
expense of free speech."[44]

The court's sympathy, I'm sure, was appreciated by the U of M
administration. Of course, all the judicial condolences in the world
won't solve the problem. Colleges are stuck between a rock and a
hard place when it comes to campus speech. The rock is the First
Amendment—a literal foundation of our government that guarantees
freedom of expression. The hard place, or places, are Title VI and Title
IX, that require schools to regulate that very expression.

SIGMA ALPHA EPSILON AT THE UNIVERSITY OF OKLAHOMA

Congratulations, you've now completed your campus free speech crash
course. Let's put what you know to use by analyzing a case that never
went to court because the expelled students never sued. As we go
through the facts think about what you've learned about the exceptions to free speech, the constitutionality of speech codes, threats,
and fighting words.

On Saturday March 7, 2015, members of Sigma Alpha Epsilon (SAE)
at the University of Oklahoma were on a bus headed to a fraternity
founders' day event. Two members, Levi Pettit and Parker Rice, led
the crowd in an unbelievably offensive song.[45] It was to the tune of
"If You're Happy and You Know It" but the words were abhorrently
racist. They sang:

There will never be a N**** at SAE

There will never be a N**** at SAE

You can hang him from a tree,

But he'll never pledge with me,

There will never be a N**** at SAE[46]

Someone filmed it. By Sunday night the 10-second clip was circulating on campus. By Monday morning protests erupted. Soon it was making national headlines.[47] SAE national headquarters revoked the chapter's charter. The fraternity house was shut and permanently banned from recolonizing. And the two students who led the chant, Rice and Pettit, were expelled from school.

I'm sure we can all agree that the song was unequivocally vile. But whether or not something is appalling isn't the test. The real question

FIGURE 1.4   Levi Pettit and Parker Rice leading a racist chant on a bus to the SAE founders' day events.

is "Was this awful song protected speech?" If Pettit and Rice had sued the school for violating their First Amendment rights, would they have won? Let's go through the law, point by point.

First, the University of Oklahoma is a public school. It's part of the government. The First Amendment applies.

Next, we have to decide whether the song falls into one of the content-based exceptions to free speech. At the outset we can easily say that the song itself isn't speech that breaks the law. It's not perjury, defamation, solicitation, or blackmail. It's also clearly not obscenity as laid out in the Miller test or child pornography.

It also fails the incitement to imminent lawless action test. Remember Brandenburg and his 12 racist cohorts out in that field in Ohio? He spoke of "revengeance," but his threats were theoretical and in the distant future and were, therefore, protected speech. The song sung by Pettit and Rice is similar. The lynching is speculative. There's no incitement here.

That leaves us with fighting words and true threats. These are closer calls. But still, the song falls outside of both. The reason: Both require that the speech be directed at someone specific. Think back to *Virginia v. Black*. The SAE incident is more analogous to the cross burned in the field than the one on the lawn of the African American couple. The bus riders were all White, and all singing along. If the facts were a little different—if Pettit and Rice had led the chant outside the window of a minority student—it might qualify as either fighting words or a threat. But as the facts stand, where the racist speech happened in closed space with no minorities in attendance, it just doesn't work.

The only possible legal justification for Pettit and Rice's expulsions would be under the auspices of Title VI of Civil Rights Act of 1964. The clip went viral. It was widely seen by all the students at the school. You could make an argument that the mere presence of students who are so blatantly racist creates an environment that wouldn't allow minorities to effectively learn. I think that's the strongest case. But content-based speech restrictions are almost always stuck down. I don't think it would hold up in court.

Chances are, if Pettit and Rice had sued, the courts would have found their expulsion in violation of the First Amendment and the school would have been ordered to re-enroll them. Would that have been perfectly fair to the entire University of Oklahoma community? Should minority students have to endure that kind of speech, or the presence of those kinds of people, on their campus? Maybe not. But as I said at the beginning of the chapter, First Amendment law is almost always an exercise in compromise.

That may leave you with a bad taste in your mouth. It does for me. I understand and agree with that outcome legally. But I hate that people could behave this way without severe consequences. That said, I'll give you a final thought that may provide some comfort, cold as it may be. On some level it makes sense to keep racists in school. Bigotry is ignorance. And the cure for that kind of stupidity is education. If you expel someone for being racist, sexist, or homophobic it practically guarantees they'll be bitter and ignorant for the rest of their lives. If they stay in school, there's a chance they'll evolve.

If an incident like this takes place on your campus I say lean into the learning and evolving side of the equation rather than the punishment part. Encourage your administration to use the incident to start a discussion. And resist the urge to cancel the offender. They may be beyond help, but at least give them a chance to grow.

CHAPTER SUMMARY

The First Amendment to the U.S. Constitution is the law that grants us the right to freely express ourselves. It only applies to government entities. Therefore, public schools must recognize your First Amendment rights. Private schools are exempt, except in California where a state law extends First Amendment protections to private colleges.

Our free speech rights aren't absolute. The government can regulate expression under certain, specific circumstances. These exemptions fall into two broad categories. The first are content based; the second are time, place, and manner restrictions. Content-based exemptions include fighting words, true threats, incitement to lawless action, obscenity, child pornography, and speech that breaks the law in and of itself—like perjury or blackmail. Over the years, the courts have laid out tests for each of the content-based exemptions. The government can also enforce time, place, and manner restrictions on speech, such as noise ordinances. Time, place and manner restrictions must be content neutral, narrowly tailored to achieve a significant government goal, and leave open alternative channels for free expression.

Some colleges have established free speech zones that restrict expression to a specific area on campus. When challenged in court, these zones are almost always found to violate the First Amendment. Similarly, some colleges have enacted speech codes in an attempt to maintain learning environments free from racist or sexist speech. Courts almost always rule that these codes violate the First Amendment.

NOTES

1   Piarowski v. Illinois Community College, 759 F.2d 625, 628 (1985).

2   Ibid., 625, 527.

3   Ibid., 625.

4   Ibid., 628.

5   Ibid., 632.

6   U.S. Constitution, First Amendment.

7   CA Educ Code § 94367 (2021).

8   Hanson, Melanie. "College Enrollment & Student Demographic Statistics." *Education Data Initiative*, 26 July 2022, https://educationdata.org/college-enrollment-statistics.

9   "Occupational Employment and Wage Statistics." U.S. Bureau of Labor Statistics, https://www.bls.gov/oes/oes_emp.htm. Accessed 10 October 2022.

10   Beiler, Des. "A Sports Writer Was Fired after Comparing Trump's Inauguration to 9/11. Now He's Suing." *Washington Post*, 8 February 2017, https://www.washingtonpost.com/news/early-lead/wp/2017/02/08/fired-after-anti-trump-tweet-sports-writer-sues-new-york-post/.

11   San Diego v. Roe, 543 U.S. 77 (2004).

12   Chaplinsky v. State of New Hampshire, 315 U.S. 568 (1942).

13   Purtell v. Mason, 527 F. 3d 615 (2008).

14   Johnson v. Campbell 332 F.3d 199 (2003).

15   State v. York, 732 A.2d 859 (1999).

16   Brandenburg v. Ohio, 395 U.S. 444, 446 (1969).

17   Ibid., 444, 445.

18   Ibid., 444, 447.

19   Virginia v. Black et al., 538 U.S. 343 (2003).

20   Ibid., 343, 348.

21   Ibid., 343, 367.

22   Jacobellis v. Ohio, 378 U.S. 184, 197 (1964).

23   Miller v. California, 413 U.S. 15 (1973).

24   Ibid., 15, 24.

25   Piarowski v. Illinois Community College, 759 F.2d 625, 627 (1985).

26   Feiner v. New York, 340 U.S. 315 (1951).

27   Healy v. James, 408 U.S. 169, 189 (1972).

28   Ward v. Rock Against Racism, 491 U.S. 781 (1989).

29   Ibid., 781, 785.

30   Ibid., 781, 791.

31   Kraft, Emilie. "Free Speech Zones." Free Speech Zones. *The First Amendment Encyclopedia*, https://mtsu.edu/first-amendment/article/960/free-speech-zones. Accessed 10 October 2022.

32   Shaw v. Burke et al. 2:17-CV-02387-ODW p. 6 (C.D. Cal.) (2018).

33   Ibid.

34   Ibid.

35   "Los Angeles Pierce College – Stand Up For Speech Lawsuit." *Foundation for Individual Rights and Expression*, 2017, https://www.thefire.org/cases/pierce-college-sufs-lawsuit/.

36   Civil Rights Act of 1964, Title VI, 42 U.S.C. § 2000d et seq. (1964).

37   Title IX of the Education Amendments of 1972, 20 U.S.C. §1681-§1688 (1972).

38   Wilson, Robert. "U. of Wisconsin Considers Proposal to Ease Limits on Faculty Speech." *Chronicle of Higher Education*, 2 October 1998, p. A-17.

39   Doe v. University of Michigan, 721 F. Supp 852 (E.D. Mich.) (1989).

40   Ibid., 852.

41   Ibid., 852, 856.

42   Ibid., 852, 858.

43   Ibid.

44   Ibid.

45   Gray, Eliza. "Racist Chant at Oklahoma University Was Ingrained by SAE Frat." *Time*, 9 March 2015, https://time.com/3761767/racist-chant-ingrained-sae/.

46   New, Jake. "Fraternity Caught on Video Singing Racist Song." *Inside Higher Ed.*, 9 March 2015, https://www.insidehighered.com/quicktakes/2015/03/09/fraternity-caught-video-singing-racist-song.

47   Svrluga, Susan. "OU: Frat Members Learned Racist Chant at National SAE Leadership Event." *Washington Post*, 27 March 2015, https://www.washingtonpost.com/news/grade-point/wp/2015/03/27/ou-investigation-sae-members-learned-racist-chant-at-national-leadership-event/.

Credits

GUEST SPEAKERS AND DIRECT DISAGREEMENT

GUEST SPEAKERS

"If there be time to expose through discussion, the falsehoods and fallacies, to avert the evil by the processes of education, the remedy to be applied is more speech, not enforced silence." Justice Brandeis wrote that nearly 100 years ago.[1] But his meaning still holds true. The best response to negative speech is more speech. When someone puts forward an idea you find abhorrent, don't silence them. Argue with them. Stand your ideas up against theirs and battle it out on the merits.

This is sometimes called the counter-speech doctrine. I think it's the single most important concept in free speech. And there's no place in the country where counter-speech should function more effectively than on a campus. If we can't discuss big, difficult, and potentially offensive topics at colleges and universities, where can we? Unfortunately, recently there's been a tendency to snuff out ideas we don't like; to ignore anything that falls outside our comfort zone; or worse, to heckle the views of those who oppose us out of existence.

Some ideas are so vile it feels wrong to legitimize them at a place of higher learning. Holocaust or Sandy Hook deniers come to mind. But most issues aren't that cut and dried. The vast majority of offensive theories are worth debating, if for no other reason to definitively prove them wrong. And even in the most extreme cases, who better than a history professor to take down a conspiracy theorist like David Irving or a journalist to dismantle Alex Jones's Sandy Hook idiocy. That's the mind-set I want you to adopt as you read this chapter: When you disagree don't silence, debate.

Murray at Middlebury

On March 2, 2017, a group of Middlebury College students taught a master class in the worst way to respond to a controversial speaker. A conservative student group at the college—the American Enterprise

Institute Club—invited Charles Murray to speak.[2] Calling Murray controversial is an understatement. In 1994 he coauthored a book titled *The Bell Curve* where he argued that intelligence is linked to race.[3] He's been labeled by the Southern Poverty Law Center as a White nationalist for using "racist pseudoscience and misleading statistics to argue that social inequality is caused by the genetic inferiority of the black and Latino communities, women, and the poor."[4]

A large swath of the American population finds his views abhorrent. But that's not the point. Some of the students at Middlebury thought what he had to say was worth hearing. They didn't want Murray's theories to go unchecked. They framed his appearance as a debate. They enlisted a liberal-leaning professor, Allison Stanger, to lead a discussion after his remarks in which she and audience members could question and challenge him.[5]

Even the publicity before the talk emphasized that they wanted attendees to verbally spar with Murray. An article that ran in the college paper before the event, written by a few members of the group, was titled "The AEI Invites You to Argue." In it the authors wrote, "Examining and engaging with a wide variety of thoughts and ideas is an essential part of what it means to pursue a liberal arts education. In this pursuit, we must as an institution encourage robust discussion and expose the Middlebury Community to diverse thoughts."[6] The AEI Club wasn't saying, "We think Murray's right; come listen to his amazing theories," but rather "This person is influential, but his ideas may be flawed; let's get him on campus and give him a run for his money."

Still, the very idea of Murray's talk stirred up resentment. More than 500 alumni signed a letter condemning his appearance before the fact calling it "unacceptable and unethical."[7] The administration, to their credit, didn't back down. They supported the AEI Club, and the program went forward. But, at the event itself, the situation devolved into chaos almost immediately.

Before the lecture even began more than 100 students stood up, turned their backs to the stage, and started to chant: "Racist, sexist, anti-gay, Charles Murray go away"; "Your message is hatred, we cannot tolerate it"; and the perennial favorite of mobs everywhere, "Hey Hey, Ho Ho, Charles Murray's got to go."[8] The shouting was loud enough to drown Murray out even with the use of a sound system. After roughly a half hour a school representative took the podium and said that if the disruptions didn't end, the lecture would be moved to an undisclosed location and livestreamed. Professor Stanger also spoke briefly saying, "I've spent a lot of time preparing really hard questions; we're going to

FIGURE 2.1   Students protest Charles Murray at Middlebury.

have a great dialogue if you let us continue." She left the stage saying, "You're not going to let us speak. I think that's a terrible shame."[9]

The talk was moved to another building, but the mob found the new location. During the livestream they pulled fire alarms in an attempt to disrupt it. When Stanger and Murray tried to leave afterward, they were surrounded by protestors. Some were in masks and may have been outside agitators, but many were Middlebury students. Stanger was assaulted. Someone pulled her and badly twisted her neck while she was trying to help Murray get to the car. Once in their vehicle, the protestors pounded on it with their fists, rocked it back and forth, and jumped on the hood. Stanger was later treated at a local hospital where she was diagnosed with a concussion and fitted with a neck brace.[10]

Shortly after the incident, the school hired an independent law firm to help identify and punish the students that were involved. In the end 67 students were disciplined but none were expelled. No one was charged criminally.[11] Middlebury's president, Laurie Patton, issued a public apology to Murray and in a later statement said, "I want to state that peaceful, non-disruptive protest is not only allowed at Middlebury, it is encouraged. We all have the right to make our voices heard, both in support of and in opposition to people and ideas. Our concern is acts of disruption and violence, where available means of peaceful protest were declined."[12] In response, Murray called the sanctions a "farce" and said, "They will not deter anyone. They're a statement to students that if you shut down a lecture, nothing will happen to you."[13]

The Heckler's Veto

The Murray incident is an extreme example. But it's not unique. Speakers are regularly shouted down at universities across the country. In September of 2022 at the University of New Mexico hundreds of protestors stopped a talk by Tomi Lahren. She ended her speech early and was escorted out of the building.[14] In March of 2022 protestors at the University of North Texas forced Texas House candidate Jeff Younger to cut his talk short.[15] Similar incidents have occurred at Columbia University, Yale, University of California (UC), Hastings, CUNY, UC Berkley, University of Oregon, University of Connecticut (UCONN), Duke, and several other schools across the country. Google "college students shout down speaker" and you'll find dozens of examples.

It's not exclusively conservative speakers that are silenced. There are instances of liberals being heckled too. In 2017 Trump supporters (most weren't students) drowned out two Democratic speakers at Whittier College with chants of "respect our president" and "America first." The talk was scheduled for an hour but ended after only 34 minutes.[16] And in a case of a left-leaning group silencing another left-leaning group, members of the local Black Lives Matter group successfully shouted down the head of the Virginia ACLU, Claire Guthrie Gastañaga in 2017 at William & Mary. She was on campus, ironically, for a talk titled "Students and the First Amendment." The members of the BLM Chapter were protesting the fact that the ACLU fights for the First Amendment rights of the Ku Klux Klan and White nationalists (among all others). They screamed "ACLU, you protect Hitler too" and "the oppressed are not impressed," forcing the talk to be cancelled.[17]

The practice of drowning out speakers with chants and protests is commonly called a heckler's veto. Statistics show that most undergrads think it's an appropriate way to respond to ideas they don't like. A 2022 survey found that 62% of college students felt that shouting down a speaker was an acceptable way to protest speech. And 20% thought that using violence to stop campus speakers was "at least rarely acceptable."[18] Those numbers are, in my opinion, incredibly troubling. I worry that so many think it's okay to silence opposing views. But that anyone, let alone a fifth of all students, think that violence is an appropriate response to speech is appalling.

Safety Cancellations

Sometimes, before a speaker even sets foot on campus, a college will revoke their invitation for safety reasons. In 2017 UC Berkeley canceled a lecture to be given by conservative commentator Ann Coulter—twice. She was originally scheduled to speak in late April. But a week before the appearance Berkeley called off the talk citing security concerns. They were, according to a university statement, "unable to find a safe and suitable venue."[19] Tentative plans were put in place to have her appear later, but those were ultimately cancelled too. Berkeley's chancellor said at the time, "While our commitment to freedom of speech and expression remains absolute, we have an obligation to heed our police department's assessment of how best to hold safe and successful events."[20]

Can a university cancel a lecture for safety reasons? As with most things legal the answer is "it depends." If there's a credible threat of violence then, of course, the school can shut things down. They have an obligation to protect the speaker, their students, and the audience. But protests that might turn violent aren't enough to merit cancellation. Berkeley probably made the right call. Outside militant groups had been targeting the campus area for months prior to Coulter's scheduled appearance. And there had been a several violent clashes leading up to the date of the talk.[21] The totality of the situation pointed toward violence. But that's not always the case.

During that same week a similar situation played out—with a different result—at Auburn University in Alabama. A non-student named Cameron Padgett rented Auburn's Foy auditorium for white nationalist Richard Spencer to speak. The administration initially supported Spencer's appearance stating, "We strongly deplore his views, which run counter to those of this institution. While his event isn't affiliated with the university, Auburn supports the constitutional right to free speech."[22]

Then, just three days before his arrival, the school recanted and called off the talk citing "legitimate concerns and credible evidence that it will jeopardize the safety of students, faculty, staff and visitors." Padgett sued the school claiming the cancellation violated his First Amendment rights. The court agreed and ordered Auburn to allow Spencer to speak. The judge reasoned that the mere possibility of violence wasn't a good enough reason to censor him.[23]

LET THEM SPEAK, BUT SPEAK UP

What should you do if a controversial speaker is invited to your campus? I say, let them come. And let them speak. The right to free speech, as you know, isn't absolute. If an invited speaker is going to make true threats, incite violence, or engage in any other kind of speech that's not protected by the First Amendment, then the college can—and should—shut them down. But in all other cases let them walk onto the stage and have their say.

Counter-Speech

You don't have to silently endure every guest speaker's ideas. Make your side of the argument known. Just do it without silencing your ideological opponent.

Q&A

Remember Brandeis' directive—the best response to negative speech is more speech. If a controversial speaker is coming to your school you should demand, at the very least, that there be a question-and-answer period following the talk. Then attend and ask pointed questions. Maybe even coordinate with other like-minded students to make sure that all bases of your side of the argument are covered.

Debate

Even better, ask that the event be a debate rather than a lecture. Think back to Middlebury. As I said, I commend the AEI club for the way they planned Murray's appearance. They understood that allowing Murray's ideas to go unchecked was wrong and arranged for the opposing view to be voiced by Allison Stanger. I also commend Murray for agreeing to share the stage with an intellectual opponent.

Competing Program

If the event organizers won't agree to a debate or even a Q&A, then consider counter programming. Invite a speaker from the other side of the spectrum and schedule their lecture for the same time slot. Or hold it a few days later so they can address, and debunk, points made in the original talk.

Protest—but Watch the Narrative

If all else fails, protest. But do so without disrupting the event. Be forceful but respectful. Don't resort to threats, intimidation, or violence. There are myriad reasons to avoid those kinds of chaos—they're illegal and against school rules for starters. More importantly, as soon as you cross the line into disorder you've lost the intellectual high ground. You'll move the focus of the story away from the ideas you're fighting and onto your behavior.

Think back to Middlebury again. Had the event gone on as planned the headline in the local paper might have read "Middlebury Professor Debates and Defeats Charles Murray." The story might have even included coverage of why his ideas are wrong. Instead, publications across the country ran headlines like "Mob Attacks Middlebury Professor and Charles Murray."

Ironically, the students at Middlebury elevated Murray to the forefront of the national consciousness. Their actions focused 10,000 times the attention on him the small stage at their school could have ever provided. Further, they handed him the ability to criticize them. Instead of having to defend his ideas, he got to talk about how the sanctions for the students weren't harsh enough. The Middlebury protestors worked against their own interests in every possible way.

By comparison, look at how a group at the University of Pennsylvania students responded to the arrival of Heather MacDonald. In September of 2017 the Federalist Society at Penn's Law School invited her to present a lecture. MacDonald is the author of a book titled "The War on Cops" and has argued, among other things, that racial discrimination in policing is a false narrative. Blacks commit more crime, she says, and the policing follows. She's also a vocal critic of the Black Lives Matter movement asserting that it's done more harm than good.[24]

When word of MacDonald's appearance got out, Penn's Black Graduate and Professional Student Assembly began to organize a protest. In response, the Penn Law administration closed the event to the general public. Only law students were allowed to attend. The associate dean for communications at Penn Law said they made the move to "ensure that the event ran smoothly and in the spirit of open dialogue."[25]

How shutting out dissenting voices serves "the spirit of open dialogue" escapes me. Especially when those who oppose you are graduate and professional students at an Ivy League school. This wasn't an unhinged uneducated mob. The other side represented some of the sharpest minds in the country.

That intelligence showed in their response. They staged a silent protest outside the building where MacDonald was speaking. Brie Starks, vice president of the Black Graduate and Professional Student Assembly, said, "There is a time for peace and there is a time

FIGURE 2.2   Students protest Heather MacDonald's appearance at the University of Pennsylvania.

for radicalism. And at this time, and the way the climate is, we didn't want to be radical. We wanted to be peaceful in our approach while also still making a statement."[26]

TALKING WITH THE "OTHER SIDE"

Guest speakers are an important part of the campus marketplace of ideas. But even under the best of circumstances—when the lecture actually takes place and is followed by a vigorous debate—it's doubtful that any minds are changed in the space of a single hour. Lectures are performances, not connections. Real understanding takes time, mutual respect, and empathy.

As a society we seem to have lost the ability to talk with each other. In the last few years, I've watched my friends divide themselves into opposing political camps. People that were once close now avoid one another due to ideological differences. And if they do get together, they avoid talking about anything real for fear of a fight. Most can't even stomach the idea that a person they regard as a friend might feel differently about abortion, Trump, marriage rights, or immigration.

It's a missed opportunity of gargantuan proportions. We need to talk to one another about issues big and small, especially with those we love and respect. In most cases, when I've engaged a friend about their beliefs—and I mean really taken the time to listen to their motivations and understand their thinking—it's ended well. We almost always find more common ground than you'd expect.

I'm hoping your generation will exceed mine (you're better at most things from what I've seen) and actually talk with one another about the things that matter to you. Seek out classmates who have different backgrounds, religions, ideologies, sexual identities, and political leanings than yours. Learn about them and what they think. Following are a few tips for making those conversations as fruitful as possible.

Leave Insults Out

The British physician John Hughlings Jackson famously wrote, "He who was the first to abuse his fellow man instead of knocking out his brains without a word, laid thereby the basis of civilisation." Jackson's quote is the more erudite version of "sticks and stones may break my bones, but words will never hurt me." Both point to the fact that speech is less harmful than violence. But the two also place physical abuse and words on the same continuum.

That's incredibly important to recognize. Although insults aren't as painful as an uppercut hook, they can still hurt. Avoid name calling and insults. More importantly, make sure nothing you say demeans your conversational partner. You may think the notion that life starts at conception is ridiculous. But that idea might be a defining value for the person you're talking with. Belittling that position could be tantamount to attacking their identity. Tread carefully when you get down to core issues. Say things like "I really don't understand that; explain it to me" rather than, "Well that just doesn't make any sense at all."

Research the Opposing View

Technology lets us exist in ideological echo chambers. Too often we only seek out information that supports what we already believe. Maddeningly, I catch myself doing this with issues both big and small.

Last year I binged the latest season of *The Marvelous Mrs. Maisel* while flying around the Midwest. I wasn't happy with how the story was progressing. After I de-planed one day, I decided to see what the critics had to say. I opened my phone and, without even thinking,

typed "Marvelous Mrs. Maisel Bad" into the prompt. I caught myself
and swapped out "reviews" for "bad." But still, I realized that I was so
invested in my opinion—about a fictional 1950s comedienne on an
Amazon Prime show—that I subconsciously sought out people who
agreed with me.

Don't fall into that trap, especially for the important issues. Seek
out sources that challenge what you think. Watch the "other" news
network once in a while. Read a newspaper that leans away from you
politically. If you're passionate about something, do a deep dive into
the other side's arguments. If nothing else, you'll to be able to better
defend what you think.

Do Your Homework

Brush up about the facts that support your position as well. Don't think
that skimming an article in *The Atlantic* or watching a documentary
or two makes you an expert. Take the time to really learn about your
cause. Remember, you're at a college. There's knowledge around every
corner. Knock on some doors and ask for guidance. I'm sure any professor would be happy to help you. At the very least they'll be able to
point you to the best sources on a given subject.

Avoid Assumptions about Others' Drivers

If you guess at the reasoning behind someone else's actions or beliefs,
you'll probably get it wrong—dead wrong. We're also all biased in an
infinite number of ways. We tend to cut ourselves slack while judging
others extremely harshly. Thomas McFall's 2018 Twitter story about
one of his classmates is a perfect example.

McFall sat in the same seat every day.[27] And every morning the
foreign student who sat next to him would have his belongings piled
high on McFall's seat.[28] When McFall would arrive, the other student
would frantically move his things, then say "You ready for class?" and
give McFall a high five.[29] It annoyed McFall to no end. He didn't want
to high five a guy he barely knew every day at the crack of dawn. And
he couldn't understand why this student insisted on using his seat as
a storage area.[30]

Then one day McFall hung back, just outside the classroom door,
to send a text before class. He could see his seat from where he stood.
As usual, the other student's stuff was on it.[31] While he was typing,
another classmate, also running a little late, tried to sit in his usual

seat. The foreign student stopped him and said, "I'm sorry, my good friend Thomas sits here."[32]

It was only then that McFall realized his neighbor wasn't trying to annoy him; he was saving his seat. He tweeted, "This whole time he saw me as a friend but I was too busy thinking about myself to take him into consideration."[33]

McFall's tale underscores a simple fact: Guessing at someone else's motivations rarely works. Avoid assumptions. Let people tell you what underlies their thoughts and deeds. If they don't, avoid the urge to fill in the blanks yourself.

Accept That You May be Wrong

You must engage with an open mind. If your starting point is "I'm right and you're wrong," the dialogue will go nowhere. Get comfortable with the possibility that you may be misinformed. You're expecting your conversational partner to potentially change what they think. Be prepared to do the same.

Don't Expect Capitulation

Along the same lines, don't expect to "win" the talk. No one's ever chatted over coffee for a half hour, then immediately reversed their entire belief system. A meaningful conversation is a victory in and of itself. The good news: A productive dialogue leads to more conversations. That's how we all change and grow—by taking the time to talk with and listen to our peers, especially the ones who think differently than we do.

JAMES MEREDITH

You may be thinking, "Why should I even try to talk to people on the other side? They'll never listen. It's not my job to try change their minds." I understand that. Look around America today and it's easy to be discouraged. We're deeply divided and, for the most part, unwilling to listen to one another. Our problems seem unsolvable.

But remember, even during the darkest eras of our history, small groups of people, and sometimes individuals, managed to break through and make significant changes. James Meredith's enrollment at the University of Mississippi is a perfect example.

In 1954 the U.S. Supreme Court ruled in *Brown v. Board of Education* that segregation in public schools was unconstitutional.[34] Still, many colleges, like the University of Mississippi, resisted integration. In 1960 their student body remained entirely White. James Meredith worked tirelessly, and put himself at significant risk, to change that.

After high school Meredith served in the U.S. Air Force for 10 years. While overseas he took college courses from the University of Kansas, Washburn University, the United States Armed Forces Institute, and the Far East Division of the University of Maryland. After his honorable discharge he attended one of Mississippi's historically Black colleges and universities (HBCUs)—Jackson State College.

In 1961 he applied as a transfer student to the University of Mississippi, or Ole Miss as it's sometimes called. There wasn't an official policy that barred people of color from attending. Still, the application process made it nearly impossible for anyone who wasn't White to get in.[35]

For the next five months the Ole Miss admissions office did everything thing they could to discourage Meredith. First, they told him his application was received after a made-up deadline.[36] In response Meredith asked that the school treat it as continuing and to use it for the 1961 summer or fall sessions. Three months later the registrar informed Meredith that the school would only be able to offer him 48 hours of credit for his prior college work, not the 90 he had submitted. Meredith immediately wrote back and agreed.[37]

On May 25th, 1961, Ole Miss officially rejected Meredith for specious reasons. They said his prior course work didn't qualify because the colleges weren't members of "regional associations." And they said his letters of recommendation weren't sufficient.[38] Meredith immediately filed suit. After a legal battle that lasted a year and half, the courts ordered Ole Miss to admit him.

In a final attempt to keep Meredith out, the governor of Mississippi, a segregationist named Ross Barnett, enacted a law that barred the university from admitting anyone convicted of a crime of "moral turpitude." Mississippi officials then had Meredith arrested and jailed on trumped up charges of voter fraud—Meredith had mistakenly written 1960 instead of 1961 when he registered to vote. Barnett also personally, physically blocked attempts by Meredith to enroll by surrounding the registration office with 200 state troopers.[39] The federal government blocked enforcement of the voting law and threatened Barnett with arrest and a $10,000-a-day fine until Meredith was enrolled.[40]

Meredith finally arrived at the University of Mississippi on September 30, 1962, accompanied by 24 federal marshals. President Kennedy also sent additional marshals and roughly 3,000 National Guard troops to Oxford in an attempt to keep the peace. It didn't work. Students were joined by thousands of racists who streamed in from around the state and country. They turned the small college town

FIGURE 2.3   James Meredith walking to class accompanied by U.S. marshals.

FIGURE 2.4   U.S. marshals at Ole Miss in October of 1962.

into a war zone. Two men died, hundreds were wounded, and millions of dollars in damage was done to campus and the surrounding area. In the end more than 30,000 troops were deployed to subdue the rioters.[41]

Still, the next day Meredith went to class. He wrote in his autobiography that the tear gas lingering in the classroom was so thick students cried during the lecture.[42]

Meredith had enough credits to graduate after two semesters. During that year he was continually harassed and ostracized by his classmates. Students banged on his doors and threw bottles at his window to disrupt his studying and keep him from sleeping. He was constantly called the N word. Students got off the sidewalk when he walked by to avoid being near him. At one point someone put a "Whites Only" sign on the water fountain in his dorm. He lived in constant danger. He was accompanied by federal marshals 24/7. And his family members across the country were threatened.[43] But he persevered, and on August 18, 1963, James Meredith became the first African American to graduate from the University of Mississippi. He later went on the get a law degree from Columbia University.

That's an abbreviated accounting of Meredith's time at Ole Miss. Still, it throws into high relief the breadth of what he was up against. He had to fight for years in court to gain admission to a college that was illegally keeping him out. Then when he finally arrived the governor, the state police, and 10,000 rioters reacted to his presence on campus with violence. After the mob was subdued, he spent a year enduring daily harassment and threats.

James Meredith is truly an extraordinary man. He was able to move the civil rights movement forward through will and perseverance. There are lots of lessons to be learned from his story. But for me the most important is this: If James Meredith could change minds—and history—in that era, certainly we can overcome what divides us today.

I'm lucky. My job puts me in contact with thousands of college students every year. Although the media often highlights the worst among you, I've seen far more accurately who you are. For every racist that marched at the University of Virginia, I know that there are countless amazing, intelligent, and caring college students. Among you, I'm sure, are hundreds of your generation's James Merediths who will work tirelessly to improve the world. I have absolute faith that you're up to the task.

CHAPTER SUMMARY

The practice of shouting down speakers so they can't be heard is called a heckler's veto. Charles Murray's appearance at Middlebury College is an extreme example. There, students not only interrupted the talk, but physically attacked Murray and the moderator afterward. There have been dozens of similar incidents at colleges across the country. Some schools have cancelled lectures ahead of time citing safety concerns. In one instance, the organizer sued the school and court mandated the lecture be held. The judge ruled that a vague possibility of violence wasn't enough to justify censorship.

Instead of drowning out controversial speakers, let them talk. Then make the case for your side. This is called the counter-speech doctrine. The remedy for offensive speech is more speech. If a controversial speaker is slated to appear at your school, ask for a debate format rather than a lecture. Or push for an extended question-and-answer period following the talk. If neither are possible, counter the program by inviting a speaker who represents the opposing view. If all else fails, protest. But do so respectfully.

While at school try to see beyond your world view. Engage with students who think differently than you do. Take a few steps to ensure the talks are fruitful. Most importantly, don't insult anyone's values. Enter the talks with an open mind and recognize that you might be wrong. And don't try to "win" the conversation. Having a meaningful exchange with someone is the victory.

Given the deep divisions in America today, it may seem futile to try to talk to the "other side." But remember, even during some of our nation's worst chapters, individuals have managed to change minds. James Meredith, who fought both legal and actual battles to attend the University of Mississippi, shows that progress can be made in any environment.

NOTES

1   Whitney v. California, 274 U.S. 357, 377 (1927).

2   Beinart, Peter. "A Violent Attack on free speech at Middlebury." *The Atlantic*, 6 March 2017, https://www.theatlantic.com/politics/archive/2017/03/middlebury-free-speech-violence/518667/.

3   Ibid.

4 "Extremist Files." *Southern Poverty Law Center*, https://www.splcenter.org/fighting-hate/extremist-files/individual/charles-murray.

5 Beinart, "A Violent Attack on Free Speech."

6 Khan, Alexander, et al. "AEI Invites You to Argue." *The Middlebury Campus*, 23 February 2017, https://www.middleburycampus.com/article/2017/02/aei-invites-you-to-argue.

7 Seelye, Katharine. "Protesters Disrupt Speech by 'Bell Curve' Author at Vermont College." *New York Times*, 3 March 2017, https://www.nytimes.com/2017/03/03/us/middlebury-college-charles-murray-bell-curve-protest.html.

8 Beinart, "A Violent Attack on Free Speech."

9 DiGravo, Will. "Students Protest Lecture by Dr. Charles Murray at Middlebury College" [Video]. YouTube, 2 March 2017, https://www.youtube.com/watch?v=a6EASuhefeI.

10 Saul, Stephanie. "Dozens of Middlebury Students Are Disciplined for Charles Murray Protest." *New York Times*, 24 May 2017, https://www.nytimes.com/2017/05/24/us/middlebury-college-charles-murray-bell-curve.html.

11 Ibid.

12 "March 6 Statement from President Laurie Patton." Middlebury News and Announcements, 6 March 2017, https://www.middlebury.edu/announcements/news/2017/03/march-6-statement-president-laurie-patton. Accessed 10 October 2022.

13 Ibid.

14 Saiz, Gabriel, and Maddie Pukite. "Students of Color Denied Entry at Turning Point Event at UNM: UNM Students Unite in Protest against Tomi Lahren Event on Campus." *The Daily Lobo*, 16 September 2022, https://www.dailylobo.com/article/2022/09/students-of-color-denied-entry-at-turning-point-event-at-unm.

15 Rose, Andy, and Caroll Alvarado. "Texas State House Candidate Fighting Child Gender-Affirming Care Is Shouted Down at a College Campus Event." *CNN*, 3 March 2022, https://www.cnn.com/2022/03/03/us/north-texas-university-protest-candidate-transgender/index.html.

16 Adams, Liam. "Pro-Trump protesters Shout Down Democrat's Speech at Whittier College." *The Chronicle of Higher Education*, 16 October 2017, https://www.chronicle.com/blogs/ticker/pro-trump-protesters-shout-down-speech-at-whittier-college.

17 Gerson, Jeannie Suk. "Donald Trump, the A.C.L.U., and the Ongoing Battle over the Legitimacy of Free Speech." *The New Yorker*, 23 April 2019, https://www.newyorker.com/news/our-columnists/

donald-trump-the-aclu-and-the-ongoing-battle-over-the-legiti-macy-of-free-speech.

18 "2022-2023 College Free Speech Rankings." *Foundation for Individual Rights and Expression*, https://rankings.thefire.org. Accessed 5 August 2022.

19 Fuller, Thomas. "Berkeley Cancels Ann Coulter Speech over Safety Fears." *New York Times*, 19 April 2017, https://www.nytimes.com/2017/04/19/us/berkeley-ann-coulter-speech-canceled.html.

20 Svrluga, Susan, et al. "Ann Coulter Speech at UC Berkeley Cancelled, Again, amid Fears for Safety." *Washington Post*, 26 April 2017, https://www.washingtonpost.com/news/grade-point/wp/2017/04/26/ann-coulter-speech-canceled-at-uc-berkeley-amid-fears-for-safety/.

21 Ibid.

22 Andrews, Travis. "Federal Judge stops Auburn from Cancel-ling White Nationalist Richard Spencer Speech. Protests and a Scuffle Greet Him." *Washington Post*, 19 April 2017, https://www.washingtonpost.com/news/morning-mix/wp/2017/04/19/federal-judge-stops-auburn-from-canceling-white-national-ists-speech-violence-erupts/.

23 Padgett v. Auburn University et. al. (3:17-CV-231-WKW (WO) (M.D. Ala.). (2017).

24 Meadows, James. "A Controversial Critic of the Black Lives Matter Movement Spoke at Penn amid Student Protests." *Daily Pennsylvanian*, 28 September 2017, https://www.thedp.com/article/2017/09/a-controversial-critic-of-the-black-lives-matter-movement-spoke-at-penn-amid-student-protests.

25 Ibid.

26 Ibid.

27 McFall, Thomas (@thomas__mcfall). Twitter post, 9 April 2018, https://twitter.com/thomas__mcfall/status/983334328620011520.

28 Ibid.

29 Ibid.

30 Ibid.

31 Ibid.

32 Ibid.

33 Ibid.

34 Brown v. Board of Education of Topeka, 347 U.S. 483 (1954).

35 Meredith v Fair, 305 F.2d 343, 345-56 (1962).

36 Ibid., 343, 347.

37 Ibid., 343, 348.

38   Ibid., 343, 347.

39   United States v. Barnett, 330 F.2d 369, 426 (1963).

40   Ibid., 369, 378.

41   Sitton, Claude. "3,000 troops Put Down Mississippi Rioting and Seize 200 as Negro Attends Classes; Ex-General Walker Is Held for Insurrection." *New York Times*, 2 October 1962, https://archive.nytimes.com/www.nytimes.com/library/national/race/100262race-ra.html.

42   Meredith, James. *Three Years in Mississippi.* Indiana University Press, 1961.

43   Ibid.

Credits

SEX

The law's relationship with sex is complicated. Our legal system acts as a both a disciplinarian and a protector. It punishes sexual misdeeds like lewd exposure and assaults. But it also guarantees some level of sexual privacy by safeguarding our autonomy to make decisions about our intimate lives. This chapter is concerned only with the former: acts that are prohibited either by statutes or school rules.

The legal standing of abortion, same-sex marriage, and other sexual rights might be this generation's defining issues. But they're far too complex to be taught as a single unit in a freshman course. You could easily spend an entire year studying the 14th Amendment and its application to personal privacy. Just comparing the reasoning in *Roe v. Wade*, which recognized a federal right to abortion,[1] and *Dobbs v. Jackson Women's Health Organization*, which overruled *Roe*,[2] would take weeks. I encourage you to learn more about these subjects and get involved. But this text isn't the place to address the law and sexual privacy.

Instead, we'll concentrate on how sex might intersect with the law in your day-to-day lives. We'll focus on what you can do personally to protect yourself and stay out of trouble. A warning: This section opens with a few lighter topics—public nudity and urination. But it gets serious quickly. Some of the later subjects can be difficult, even triggering. If at any time the information is too much for you, step back and take a break. If you need to, seek out a friend or counselor for support.

---

1   Roe v. Wade, 410 U.S. 113 (1973)

2   Dobbs v. Jackson Women's Health Organization, 597 U.S. _____ (2022)

3 SEX CRIMES

Streaking to Stalking

PUBLIC NUDITY

Getting naked in public doesn't seem to be your generation's thing. In the 70s streaking on college campuses was all the rage. One study documented more than 1,000 streaking incidents at U.S. colleges in the spring semester of 1974 alone.[1] Thankfully that fad ended quickly. Still, it's wise to understand public nudity laws.

Intent

Every state has its own statute that deals with public indecency. In most jurisdictions simply being unclothed wouldn't violate indecency

    A streaker parachutes onto the University of Illinois campus in December of 1974.

laws, although it would qualify as disorderly conduct. Indecency statutes generally require some level of intent or an extenuating circumstance for the nudity to be illegal. The three most common are (1) performing a sex act in public, (2) being naked with a sexual motivation, or (3) nudity that's likely to offend others. Let's look at a few examples.

The Kansas law states the following:

> Lewd and lascivious behavior.
>
> (a) Lewd and lascivious behavior is:
>
> > (1) Publicly engaging in otherwise lawful sexual intercourse or sodomy with knowledge or reasonable anticipation that the participants are being viewed by others; or
> >
> > (2) publicly exposing a sex organ or exposing a sex organ in the presence of a person who is not the spouse of the offender and who has not consented thereto, with intent to arouse or gratify the sexual desires of the offender or another.
>
> (b) Lewd and lascivious behavior is a:
>
> > (1) Class B nonperson misdemeanor, if committed in the presence of a person 16 or more years of age; and
> >
> > (2) severity level 9, person felony, if committed in the presence of a person under 16 years of age.[2]

Part (a)(1) makes it illegal to have sex in public. Reasonable enough. Part (a)(2) contains the intent clause. It's illegal to be naked "with the intent to arouse or gratify the sexual desires of the offender or another." Part (b) upgrades the crime to a felony if someone under 16 is present. That's common. Most states increase the penalties if the audience includes minors or children.

South Dakota's law is similar but adds another layer. There, as in Kansas, it's illegal to expose one's privates with an intent to arouse. It's also against the law to be naked in public "under circumstances in which that person knows that person's conduct is likely to annoy, offend, or alarm another person."[3]

Vermont's statute doesn't say much at all:

> Lewd and lascivious conduct
>   A person guilty of open and gross lewdness and lascivious behavior shall be imprisoned not more than five years or fined not more than $300.00, or both.[4]

Vermont juries then decide what rises to the level of "lewd and lascivious" on a case-by-case basis.[5]

Indiana is the only state where simply being naked is explicitly illegal. There are multiple levels of indecency covered in their statutes, including offenses much like the ones laid out in Kansas's and South Dakota's laws. The lowest level infraction, though, is misdemeanor public nudity:

> (b) A person who knowingly or intentionally appears in a public place in a state of nudity commits public nudity, a Class C misdemeanor.[6]

My favorite law is Alaska's. There, indecent exposure in the second degree makes it illegal to expose your private parts "with reckless disregard for the offensive, insulting, or frightening effect the act may have."[7] If your genitals are insulting keep them to yourself.

Public nudity statutes may seem funny when spelled out in print, but an indecency conviction can be serious. Being found guilty could mean fines, jail time, and even inclusion on the sex offense registry. Don't take these laws lightly.

PUBLIC URINATION

Unlike public nudity, which is governed by state laws, public urination is regulated at the municipal level. Not every town has a law in place, but most do, especially college towns. In Iowa City (home of the University of Iowa) the municipal code states the following:

> 8-5-13: PUBLIC URINATION AND DEFECATION:
>
> A. It shall be unlawful for any person to urinate or defecate in or upon any street, alley, public place or in any place open to public view, provided this subsection shall not apply to restrooms or public facilities designated for such purpose.[8]

Look at how the law defines public: "any street, alley, public place or in any place open to public view." Those last six words, "any place open to public view," are important. You don't actually have to be standing on state property to be charged. As long as you can be seen from a public place, you've violated the law. Not every law includes that kind of language. Still, judges often interpret less-inclusive statutes broadly and rule against urinators who pee openly, but on privately owned land, despite what the actual law says.

In municipalities without a law that specifically addresses urination, you'd be charged under the local disorderly conduct statute. Mattoon, Illinois's (home of Eastern Illinois University) disorderly statute says, "No person shall disturb the peace, or shall be guilty of any violent, tumultuous, offensive, or disorderly conduct."[9] Peeing in the streets is certainly "offensive" and "disorderly."

The obvious next question is "Could I get charged with public indecency for urinating in public?" Based on the laws, I don't think you should. That doesn't mean you won't.

This is where intent clauses come into play. When someone urinates in public, they aren't exposing their genitals to gratify their sexual desires. They just have to pee. There's a stronger case to be made that publicly urinating would annoy, offend, or alarm another person. But even that's a stretch, especially in situations where the party relieving themselves makes an effort to conceal what they're doing, like heading into the woods to find a tree.

But that's just my opinion. I tell college students this all the time: The law is malleable. It's whatever the judge you're standing in front of says it is. And on any given day, especially in a college town in which the magistrate could be tired of dealing with unruly college kids, you might end up in front of someone who thinks differently than I do.

A case from Indiana, *Townsend v. State*, illustrates this well. A South Bend police officer saw Mr. Townsend walking down the street with his "knees held closely together." Townsend ducked behind a nearby gas station and, according to the arresting officer, looked over his shoulder suspiciously while heading around the corner. The cop followed him and found Townsend facing the wall with his hands near his groin. When the officer spoke it startled Townsend who turned around. His fly was unzipped and there was a wet spot on his pants. There was also urine on the ground and the lower part of the wall.[10]

South Bend didn't have a public urination law in place at the time, so the police charged Townsend with public indecency. He challenged his conviction in an appeals court and won. In the opinion (and this might be the best piece of legal writing ever produced) the judge wrote this:

> We conclude that the evidence is sufficient only to draw the inference that Townsend urinated in a public place; no evidence directly or circumstantially establishes that Townsend exposed his penis while doing so. Indeed, the evidence does not even establish that Townsend had a penis, much less that he knowingly or intentionally exposed it. ... Here, Townsend was convicted for urinating in a public place, not for exposing his penis to anyone. The Indiana General Assembly may choose to prohibit public urination. To date, it has not done so.[11]

I agree with the appeals court. Public urination and public indecency are different offenses and should be treated as such. But some judges and police officers might not see things that way. The ramifications of a public indecency conviction can be severe and could even lead to inclusion on the sex offense registry. Any time you relieve yourself outside you run the risk of serious legal trouble. Please, pee inside.

STALKING

Jennifer Paulson of Tacoma, Washington, met Jed Waits in the early 2000s in college at Seattle Pacific University. They were little more than acquaintances while at school. They both worked in the cafeteria and had a few friends in common. That was the extent of their relationship.[12] Still, somehow, Waits developed an unhealthy obsession with Paulson that lasted for a decade and ultimately led to her murder.

After they both graduated, Waits occasionally contacted Paulson. Early on his behavior was odd but low key. He'd phone Paulson once or twice a year. But on those days, he'd call or 10 or 15 times, sometimes as early as 5:00 a.m. In 2008 the situation escalated. Waits unexpectedly showed up at the elementary school where Paulson taught. He entered the building but was stopped by a secretary. "I never told him where I work and do not know how he found out," Paulson said at the time. Later he sent roses and a stuffed bear to the school. After that Paulson obtained a court order barring Waits from coming within 1,000 feet of her, her home, or the school.[13]

Sadly, laws and court orders don't matter to people who don't care about them. In February 2010, just a few days before she was killed,

Paulson saw Waits in the school parking lot as she left. She called 911 from her car, and the police arrested him for violating the restraining order. He was released on $10,000 bail the next day. A week later, on Friday morning, Waits waited for Paulson outside the school. As she got out of her car and walked toward the building, he shot her multiple times at point blank range.[14]

There's a lot to unpack in Paulson's case. Foremost, the justice system failed miserably. Waits was obviously a serious threat. His behaviors alone indicated that he had the potential to harm Paulson. He also had a history of mental illness. He had been discharged from the National Guard in 2007 based in part on a finding that he had a "personality not compatible with service."[15] He shouldn't have been released on bail after violating the no contact order.

Also, the laws—and therefore the tools the police and the courts had at their disposal to protect Paulson—were sorely inadequate at the time. Early stalking statutes didn't work well. Most required that the stalker make a credible threat of bodily harm before legal action could be taken. That's problematic. Stalkers rarely explicitly threaten their targets.

Thankfully, Paulson's case and others like it have led to changes in how the justice system deals with stalkers. Most current statutes require only that the stalker's actions make the victim fear for their safety or cause them emotional distress. At the time of writing only two states—Massachusetts and Arkansas—still require an explicit threat to trigger protections. Hopefully those laws will be updated soon.

There's also been a shift toward ensuring the safety of the victims above all else. After her death, Washington State passed the Jennifer Paulson Stalking Protective Order Act that gave courts better methods to protect stalking victims.[16] Many other states have tightened their laws recently.

Still, despite improved laws and increased awareness on the part of law enforcement stalking is incredibly common among college students. A 2020 survey found that 6% of students, graduate and undergrad, were stalked while at school. The numbers vary by group. Undergraduate trans, genderqueer, and nonconforming students were the most often targeted, at 15.2%. Undergrad women were the next highest at 10%. Men reported the lowest rates—3.1% for undergrads and 1.8% for graduate men.[17] Since so many cases go unreported, it's hard to pinpoint the prevalence. I suspect the true numbers are substantially higher.

The structure of college life enables stalkers. As Patrick Brady, an expert in criminal justice, said, for stalkers a campus is "kind of like

Disneyworld—you basically know where a victim is at all times."[18] Think about your life at school. How hard would it be for someone to figure out where you'll be at any given time? Student schedules are repetitive. People walk to and from the classes on set timetables, usually along the same route. They eat in the cafeterias at the same time every day. Athletes are particularly easy to track. Practice schedules and game times are published. Campuses are also open to the public and usually have excellent, free Wi-Fi coverage—making electronic stalking easier.

And, as we saw with Jennifer Paulson, stalking is often a precursor to violence. One study showed that 76% of women who were killed by their intimate partner had been stalked by the perpetrator in the year prior.[19] Think about what that means. In three quarters of the cases that involved a woman being killed by her partner or spouse, she had been stalked by the murderer—and reported it—in the preceding 12 months. Stalking is a red flag behavior. It shows that the actor has stopped making rational decisions and could be capable of much worse.

How Stalking Laws Work

Here's Texas's stalking law. It's a good example of how these statutes are written:

§ 42.072. Stalking

(a) A person commits an offense if the person, on more than one occasion and pursuant to the same scheme or course of conduct that is directed specifically at another person, knowingly engages in conduct that:

(1) constitutes an offense under Section 42.07, or that the actor knows or reasonably should know the other person will regard as threatening:

(A) bodily injury or death for the other person;

(B) bodily injury or death for a member of the other person's family or household or for an individual with whom the other person has a dating relationship; or

(C) that an offense will be committed against the other person's property;

(2) causes the other person, a member of the other person's family or household, or an individual with whom

the other person has a dating relationship to be placed in fear of bodily injury or death or in fear that an offense will be committed against the other person's property, or to feel harassed, annoyed, alarmed, abused, tormented, embarrassed, or offended; and

    (3) would cause a reasonable person to:
        (A) fear bodily injury or death for himself or herself;

        (B) fear bodily injury or death for a member of the person's family or household or for an individual with whom the person has a dating relationship;

        (C) fear that an offense will be committed against the person's property; or

        (D) feel harassed, annoyed, alarmed, abused, tormented, embarrassed, or offended.[20]

This is a comprehensive law. It contains all the common elements of stalking statutes.

Intentional

The introductory paragraph states that the stalker has to "knowingly engage in conduct." Every law has a requirement like this. Stalking has to be intentional, not coincidental or accidental.

Continuing

Look at the very first phrase in the law: "A person commits an offense if the person, on more than one occasion and pursuant to the same scheme or course of conduct." Stalking requires multiple acts, not a single act.

Threats

Parts (1), (2), and (3) discuss the effects those acts need to have on the victim or their associates. Part (1) is the threat component. But notice that it doesn't require an explicit threat. Instead, acts that the stalker "knows or reasonably should know the other person will regard as threatening" are enough to trigger the law. And note that it's not just bodily threats that count. Threats against property are included as well (§42.07 is Texas's harassment law; anything included there qualifies).

Emotional Distress

Part (2) further defines the threat requirement and adds an emotional suffering component. If the stalker's actions cause the victim "to feel harassed, annoyed, alarmed, abused, tormented, embarrassed, or offended," the law applies.

Reasonable Person

Finally, look at part (3). This section states that the stalking victim doesn't have to actually embody the fear or other emotions set out as standards themselves. If a "reasonable person" would feel those things then it's stalking, and illegal.

Find your state's stalking statute. Chances are many, if not all, of the components of the Texas law will be included. The wording may be different, but the logical structure should be very similar. Also find the rules that prohibit stalking in your student handbook. It will probably be written in much plainer language. But the general structure will be the same.

As an example, here's Denison University's stalking language:

> 6. Stalking
>
> The term "stalking" means engaging in a course of conduct directed at a specific person that would cause a reasonable person with similar characteristics under similar circumstances to fear for their safety or the safety of others; or to suffer substantial emotional distress. A course of conduct includes two or more acts, including but not limited to, those in which the alleged perpetrator directly, indirectly, or through third parties, by any action, method, device, or means, follows, monitors, observes, surveils, threatens, or communicates to or about the Complainant, or interferes with the Complainant's property. Stalking governed by Title IX refers to stalking that is sex or gender based.[21]

This is a good policy. It covers all the main points: intentional, continuing, threats, emotional distress, and reasonable person.

Technology and Stalking

A 2019 survey by the department of justice found that stalkers used technology to harass or track their victims in 80% of cases.[22] Many states have amended their laws to include electronic activity. Wyoming recently added the following to the list of prohibited activities:

> Using any electronic, digital or global positioning system device or other electronic means to place another person under surveillance or to surveil another person's internet or wireless activity without authorization from the other person.[23]

Statutes without tech-specific language would still cover electronic stalking. Using an Apple AirTag to track an ex's whereabouts, for example, would be invasive and disturbing enough to put any reasonable person into a state of emotional distress.

If You're Being Stalked

First and foremost, get safe. If you think you're in immediate danger, call 911 and find a public space or another person. Do whatever's necessary to ensure your safety.

School or Police (or Both)

In the longer term you've got two main ways to deal with a stalker. Actually, you've got the same option via two venues. You can seek relief through the school's disciplinary system, or you could pursue the stalker through the court system. And, of course, you can do both.

Schools have vast amounts of power to regulate their students and campuses when safety is at stake. And they can respond more quickly than the court system. Therefore, the college disciplinary system is probably your best, first step. Your school will be able to make sure the stalker can't be near you. If the stalker is a student they can change class schedules, put restrictions on dining hall access, and even change living arrangements while they're investigating. It's also easy for an administration to ban non-students from entering university property.

But colleges have a limited ability to enforce rules or monitor actions off campus. My advice, then, is to avail yourself of the protections offered by both the school and the court system. Go to the university first. The Title IX coordinator is a good person to contact, but any school employee you trust will work. Let them know what's going on and ask for their help. The school will be able to take immediate steps to ensure your safety, and they'll be able to help you navigate the legal system.

Protective Orders

Both the school and the court system will put some kind of protective order in place. The steps of the process will be much the same regardless of the venue—a complaint followed by an investigation, and finally a decision about the protective order. Of course, it will be much more formal in the court system. You'll have more paperwork to fill out, you might have to sign a sworn affidavit. You may even have to appear before a judge and testify before the order can be put in place. Don't be intimidated by any of this. The university and local law enforcement will help you.

If the school or the judge decides the rules or the law, respectively, have been broken, they'll issue some kind of order. In the case of the court, it will be specific. The college order may be less precise. But they'll both aim to accomplish the same thing—protecting you.

Communicate Your Fear

When initially reporting the stalking, don't downplay your emotions. The urge to minimize what's going on, to project that it's nothing you can't handle, is understandable. This isn't the time for that. Remember, the fact that you, as the target, are in fear or suffering emotional distress is an element of the crime.

Check Your Tech

At all points during the process—before, during, and after seeking a protective order—be mindful about technological invasions of your privacy. Change passwords regularly. Scan your phone and computer for malware (Apple's new iOS has a security check feature built in). Audit your online accounts to see if there have been any strange logons. Keep your software updated (to make sure security fixes and patches are all installed). If you can afford it, consider starting fresh. Just get a new phone.

The Time Surrounding Filing Can Be Dangerous

Stalkers aren't rule followers. Even if you have a protective order in place, you still need to take steps to protect yourself. This is especially true just before, and after, getting an anti-stalking order. You've taken a legal swing at someone who has demonstrated an inability to make rational decisions. Be extra cautious. Surround yourself with friends.

Stay at their house. Avoid being outside by yourself. Do what it takes to ensure you're invulnerable to attacks.

Report ALL Infractions

Stalkers push boundaries. If you let them slip by at one level, they'll likely go to the next. If he calls and you don't report it, he might show up where you work. Or, if you see her at your job and don't do anything about it, the next time she might be at your house. It's critical that you report every infraction. The limits imposed on your stalker by the school or the courts were put there for a reason. Don't let any of them slide.

The Authorities Will Believe You

If you report a violation of the protective order to the police, they will believe you. The school will too. You're not under any obligation to provide evidence. Never put yourself in harm's way to try to gather proof of what happened. You won't need a picture or anything of that nature to show the authorities. The best thing you can do is just keep notes—the time, date, and other details—to make sure you remember the facts correctly. What you say will be taken at face value.

CHAPTER SUMMARY

State laws govern public indecency. Almost all require more than simple nudity. Generally, a person must be naked in public with an intent to arouse or under circumstances that would offend others to be guilty. A conviction could mean inclusion on the sex offense registry. Public urination laws, on the other hand, are municipal. Each town has their own law. Public urination is a much less serious crime. Usually it's a summary offense, like a traffic ticket. People who urinate in public probably shouldn't be charged with public indecency. They're different offenses. But often the justice system confuses the two.

Stalking is common on college campuses. It's also often a precursor to physical violence, as in Jennifer Paulson's case. Stalking laws vary by state, but most require that the stalker's actions would make a reasonable person fearful or suffer emotional distress. Technology factors into most modern stalking cases. Some states have amended their statutes to include tech-specific language. Your college will have its own stalking policy, which should contain similar requirements.

Stalking protective orders are the main tool used to protect victims. After showing a violation of stalking laws, a court will issue an order that prohibits the stalker from contacting or being near their target. A college can do the same, but its enforcement will be limited to school-owned property. Stalkers often ignore these orders. It's important for anyone being stalked to take steps to protect themselves, especially in the time just before and after filing for a protective order. The victim should also report all infractions of the order. Stalkers will keep pushing boundaries. If they're allowed to slip by at one level, they'll likely go to the next.

NOTES

1   Aguirre, B.E., et al. "The Collective Behavior of Fads: The Characteristics, Effects and Career of Streaking." *American Sociological Review*, vol 53, 1988, 569–584.

2   KS Stat § 21–5513 (2021).

3   SD Codified L § 22-24-1.2 (2021).

4   13 V.S.A. § 2601.

5   State v. Maunsell, 170 Vt. 543, 544 (1999).

6   IN Code § 35-45-4-1.5 (2021).

7   AK Stat § 11.41.460 (2021).

8   Iowa City Municipal Code §8-5-13.

9   Mattoon Illinois Municipal Code §133.01.

10   Townsend v. State, 750 N.E.2d 416, 417 (2001).

11   Ibid., 416, 419.

12   Onstot, Laura. "Why Waits? A Murder-Suicide Involving Two Former SPU Classmates Shocks the Killer's Acquaintances, Save One." *Seattle Weekly*, 15 June 2010, https://www.seattleweekly.com/news/why-waits/.

13   Associated Press. "Teacher Stalked, Shot Dead at Wash. School." *CBS News*, 26 February 2010, https://www.cbsnews.com/news/teacher-stalked-shot-dead-at-wash-school/. Accessed 10 October 2022.

14   Onstot, "Why Waits?".

15   Ibid.

16   Associated Press. "Inslee Signs Stalking Protection Order Bill." *Herald,net*, 27 April 2013, https://www.heraldnet.com/news/inslee-signs-stalking-protection-order-bill/. Accessed 11 October 2022.

17 Cantor, David, et al. "Report on the AAU Campus Climate Survey on Sexual Assault and Misconduct." *Association of American Universities*, 2020.

18 Svokos, Alexandra. "College Students Are More Likely to Be Stalked but Less Likely to Report It, Study Finds." *Huffington Post*, 4 January 2015, https://www.huffpost.com/entry/college-students-stalked_n_6472818.

19 McFarlane, Judith, et al. "Stalking and Intimate Partner Femicide." *Homicide Studies*, vol. 3, no. 4, 1999, pp. 300–316. doi:10.1177/1088767999003004003.

20 TX Penal Code § 42.072 (2021).

21 "Sex Discrimination and Sexual Misconduct Policy." *Denison University*, 2022, https://denison.edu/forms/sex- discrimination-and-sexual-misconduct-policy.

22 Morgan, Rachel, and Jennifer Truman. "Criminal Victimization, 2019." *U.S. Department of Justice, Office of Justice Programs, Bureau of Justice Statistics*, September 2020. https://bjs.ojp.gov/content/pub/pdf/cv19.pdf.

23 WY Stat § 6-2-506 (2021).

Credit

Fig. 3.1: Source: https://www.youtube.com/watch?v=WjJeK-TPAhg.

TITLE IX AND SEXUAL ASSAULT

TITLE IX

Title IX is the law that protects students from gender discrimination. On its face, the main part of the law seems simple:

> No person in the United States shall, on the basis of sex, be excluded from participation in, be denied the benefits of, or be subjected to discrimination under any educational program or activity receiving Federal financial assistance.[1]

Title IX has a long, complicated history. It's been modified and amended, either through legislation or guidance from the Department of Education, many times over the last 50 years. There have also been dozens of lawsuits that have changed the contours of its application.

Most colleges in the U.S. are bound by Title IX. "Federal financial assistance" means any government support, direct or indirect. If a single student at a school gets a federal loan to attend, that college needs to comply with Title IX. There are a handful of schools—less than 50 nationally—that operate entirely without government money. They aren't bound by these regulations. Also, institutions that are controlled by a religious organization don't have to comply with the parts of the law that conflict with their religious tenets.

Equality in the Classroom and Beyond

If you tried to restate Title IX in its simplest form, you might end up with "schools have to treat women and men equally." In the academic arena that's relatively easy to achieve. A college couldn't ban women from taking science classes, for example. Or, if a university built a state-of-the-art lab, they couldn't restrict its use to female students and make men study in older, less-advanced spaces. In both cases the college would be treating people differently based on their gender.

If you move away from the classroom, though, equality gets harder to measure. Consider sports. Should equivalence be defined financially? In 2021 the University of Alabama spent $58 million on their football program.[2] Do they need to spend that much on a women's team? What about facilities? Do they have to build a 100,000-seat stadium for the softball team? For that matter, does there need to be a women's football program to truly make things fair? The answer to all these questions is "of course not."

Over the last 50 years the Department of Education has developed a complex set of tests to ensure women and men have equitable athletic opportunities. The government looks at multiple factors to determine if the programs are fair: Is the distribution of scholarship money between the sexes proportional? Do the sports offered align with the student body's interests and abilities? Will the differences in men's and women's facilities affect the overall quality of the program? By evaluating questions like these, the government makes a judgment call about "equality" in athletic departments. See how complicated this gets?

How, then, do we make the leap from classwork and sports teams to sexual harassment and violence? Think more broadly about the equal access that Title IX guarantees. What if your teacher's assistant (TA) was constantly hitting on you? You've politely declined the advances, but the propositions continue relentlessly. Eventually the situation would affect your ability to participate in the class. You might even want to drop the course altogether. That harassment would have affected your ability to get an education.

WHAT VIOLATES TITLE IX

→ Unequal access to an educational program—sports, classes, or any other academic or extracurricular program

→ Hostile environments—pervasive sexual or sexist conditions, like a TA constantly asking you out, or a professor making sexual or sexist jokes

→ Quid pro quo harassment (i.e., date me and I'll give you an A)

→ Sexual violence

→ Violations can occur in any gender combination—male to female, female to male, male to male, female to female

Now go one step further and consider sexual violence and its aftermath. The long-term psychological damage of a sexual assault is devastating—PTSD, depression, self-harm, dissociation, and panic attacks are all common among survivors. Dealing with any one of those conditions would make it nearly impossible to thrive at college. Letting sexual violence go unchecked at a university is, therefore, a form of discrimination that violates Title IX. The only truly equal campus is one without sexual assaults.

CONSENT

Every sexual assault statute is, at its base, about consent. This is part of Texas' law:

> Sec. 22.011. SEXUAL ASSAULT.
>
> (a) A person commits an offense if:
>
> > (1) the person intentionally or knowingly:
> >
> > > (A) causes the penetration of the anus or sexual organ of another person by any means, without that person's consent;
> > >
> > > (B) causes the penetration of the mouth of another person by the sexual organ of the actor, without that person's consent; or
> > >
> > > (C) causes the sexual organ of another person, without that person's consent, to contact or penetrate the mouth, anus, or sexual organ of another person, including the actor;[3]

The statute then defines consent:

> (b) A sexual assault under Subsection (a)(1) is without the consent of the other person if:
>
> > (1) the actor compels the other person to submit or participate by the use of physical force, violence, or coercion;
> >
> > (2) the actor compels the other person to submit or participate by threatening to use force or violence against the other person or to cause harm to the

other person, and the other person believes that the
actor has the present ability to execute the threat;

(3) the other person has not consented and the actor
knows the other person is unconscious or physically
unable to resist;

(4) the actor knows that as a result of mental disease or
defect the other person is at the time of the sexual
assault incapable either of appraising the nature of
the act or of resisting it;

(5) the other person has not consented and the actor
knows the other person is unaware that the sexual
assault is occurring;

(6) the actor has intentionally impaired the other person's power to appraise or control the other person's
conduct by administering any substance without
the other person's knowledge;

(7) the actor compels the other person to submit or
participate by threatening to use force or violence
against any person, and the other person believes
that the actor has the ability to execute the threat;[4]

Some statutes don't explicitly mention consent. But the concept is
implied throughout. Minnesota's law states the following:

609.344 CRIMINAL SEXUAL CONDUCT IN THE
THIRD DEGREE.

Subdivision 1. Adult victim; crime defined. A person
who engages in sexual penetration with another person
is guilty of criminal sexual conduct in the third degree
if any of the following circumstances exists:

(a) the actor uses coercion to accomplish the penetration;
(b) the actor knows or has reason to know that the
complainant is mentally impaired, mentally incapacitated, or physically helpless;
(c) the actor uses force, as defined in section 609.341,
subdivision 3, clause (2); or
(d) at the time of the act, the actor is in a prohibited
occupational relationship with the complainant.[5]

Every situation described in the Minnesota law denotes a lack of consent.
There's no consent when force is used. If the perpetrator is in a prohibited

relationship with the survivor (e.g., a counselor or medical provider) there can't truly be consent. And, if the survivor was mentally incapacitated at the time, they couldn't have knowingly agreed to sexual contact.

That situation, lack of consent due to incapacitation, accounts for the vast majority of cases I see on college campuses. Certainly, all kinds of sexual assaults happen at schools. But most come down to one person not being able to agree to sex because they had drugs or alcohol in their system.

Your School's Policy

The court system and the on-campus disciplinary system are completely different entities. Many of the cases adjudicated on campus couldn't be successfully prosecuted in the actual legal system. This is due to the higher standard of proof required and the more stringent rules of evidence in the court system. Therefore, your school's rules are the most important when it comes to sexual interaction. Find your college's sexual assault policy. The concept of consent will figure largely into how it's written.

As an example, this is how the University of Vermont defines sexual assault:

> Sexual Assault: A sexual act that occurs (1) without consent of the other person, or (2) by threatening or coercing the other person, or (3) by placing the other person in fear that any person will suffer imminent bodily injury.[6]

Their rules go on to define consent in detail:

Consent: A person's willingness to engage in a specific sexual act or form of sexual contact.

- → Consent is an understandable exchange of affirmative words or actions, which indicate a willingness to participate in mutually agreed upon sexual activity, in the context of all the circumstances. Consent may be revoked or withdrawn any time.
- → Consent is specific to particular sexual activity, and is absent when the activity in question exceeds the scope of consent given. It is the responsibility of the person who wants to engage in the sexual activity to ensure that they have consent from any other person engaging in sexual activity or contact. The existence of a dating relationship or a past sexual relationship

> between the persons engaging in sexual activity or contact is
> not a sufficient basis to assume consent.
>
> → Consent cannot be gained by threat, force, coercion, or intim-
>   idation, or by ignoring words or actions that indicate a lack of
>   consent or objection to the activity. Consent cannot be gained
>   by taking advantage of the incapacitation of another where
>   the Respondent knows or reasonably should have known of
>   such incapacitation. An essential element of consent is that
>   it be freely given. Freely given consent may not be present or
>   possible in relationships of a sexual or intimate nature between
>   individuals where one individual has power, supervision, or
>   authority over another.
>
> → Individuals under the age of 16 are incapable of providing con-
>   sent to sexual activity under this Policy.[7]

This is an excellent policy. The first bullet point alone sums up so much. Read it and carefully consider what it means. In my opinion, the phrase "mutually agreed upon sexual activity" is the most important. Many of us were taught that physical intimacy is about persuasion, or even pressure—getting someone to hook up with you. The blurring of that line, between seduction and coercion, is at the root of a lot our problems. I don't even like the word *seduction* because it denotes, to some extent, manipulating someone into being physical.

Change your mind-set. Approach sexual encounters as the University of Vermont policy describes—two people, deciding together, how far they want to go. Keep the mutually agreed mind-set at the core of your romantic interactions and you'll be on the right side of the law, your school's rules, and ethics.

Date Rape Drugs

Because sexual assaults often go unreported it's hard to know how often drug-facilitated sexual assaults (DFSAs) occur. The classic case—where someone slips a debilitating drug into an unknowing target's drink—probably happens less often than media coverage suggests.[8] Still, protecting yourself is critical.

Never Leave a Drink Unattended

Always keep your drink with you. Setting it down creates an opportunity for someone to slip something into it.

If You Lose Sight of It, Throw It Out

If you lose track of your drink at any point, dump it and get another. It's not worth the risk.

Don't Accept Drinks from People You Don't Know

If you do accept a drink from a stranger, don't let them bring it to you from the bar. That gives them too much time alone with your beverage. Go to the bar yourself. Order the drink and watch the bartender make it.

Don't Drink out of Communal Bowls

Taking a drink from a big bowl of punch is dangerous in many ways. Anyone could have dropped something into it. And, even if it's just alcohol, you can't know what the ratios are. Is it 20% booze? Forty? Seventy? You could easily end up getting drunker than you intended.

Remember, Anything Can Be Spiked

Drugs can be slipped into any drink, even a water bottle. Nondrinkers need to keep their guards up.

If Anything Seems Off, Act Quickly

If you sense anything wrong, either with your drink or yourself, take steps to ensure your safety. If your beverage tastes funny (especially salty), throw it out. If you feel like you're getting drunker than expected, tell a friend and get some help.

Know the Limits of Tests

There are many date rape drug tests on the market. Coasters, paper tabs, straws, and even fingernail polish have all been designed to test for some of the more common DFSA substances. Relying on one of these to protect yourself is problematic. First, drugs in circulation change constantly. An older test (or a defective one) could lead to a false sense of security. More importantly, the number-one date rape drug has always been, and will always be, alcohol—and to a lesser extent drugs—that the survivor willingly drank or took.

Alcohol and Consent

How Much Alcohol Is Too Much?

I wish I could give you a definitive rule. But consent doesn't work that way. Think of the two ends of the incapacitation spectrum. We would all agree that if someone took one sip of a drink, just to taste it, that wouldn't affect their ability to knowingly consent. It's equally obvious that someone who's passed out can't consent to any kind of sexual contact. Somewhere between those two scenarios is a line. In an on-campus hearing, that line will be determined on a case-by-case basis. A good rule of thumb is, if you're wondering at all, they've had too much.

What If We Were Both Drinking?

Students often think that if both parties were drunk, that somehow changes the calculation. It doesn't. If both parties were compromised, both could get charged with violating the school's sexual assault policy.

What If They Consented and Then We Drank?

Consent needs to be contemporary. A yes two days, two hours, or even two minutes ago doesn't necessarily connote consent—even more so if there was drinking between the consent and the act. You need knowing consent at the time of contact.

SUMMING UP CONSENT

Get a Verbal Yes

Most college policies allow for consent to be communicated through a word or an action, like a nod. Why leave any room for misinterpretation? At every step of your hookup, ask "Do you want to do x?" and wait for an answer.

Sometimes Consent Can't Be Given

Consent must be knowing, meaning made with a clear head. If the other person has drugs or alcohol in their system that impairs their ability to think, they can't consent.

Nothing Makes Consent Automatic

If you've had sex with your partner 100 times before, it doesn't mean you have permission now. If they said yes yesterday, if they

(continued)

said yes two hours ago, even if they said yes two minutes ago, that doesn't mean they've agreed in the moment.

Consent Can Always Be Withdrawn

Everyone has the right to change their mind at any point during a hookup. If your partner withdraws consent, stop immediately.

IF YOU'VE BEEN ASSAULTED

It will be nearly impossible to think clearly in the aftermath of such a traumatic event. But the hours and days after an assault are critical for your health and your ability to seek justice. First and foremost, get medical treatment. You'll be in shock. You may not realize the extent of your injuries. It's important to see a medical professional as soon as you can.

Second, you'll need to decide about having a forensic sexual assault examination, sometimes called a rape kit. You'll need to make up your mind quickly. DNA evidence will be the most important in the courts (although it rarely comes into play in on-campus hearings). It isn't viable for long—72 hours at the most. While you're deciding, don't do anything that might damage the DNA. Don't shower or bathe, douche, brush your teeth, smoke, drink or eat, or wash your hands. If possible don't change your clothes. If you do, place them in a paper bag. Storing them in a plastic bag could compromise the DNA.

I used to believe that every survivor should have the forensic exam. My legally trained mind was hell-bent on seeing justice served and preserving as many options as possible. My thinking has evolved. A forensic exam may add another level of trauma for some survivors. Shielding them from further pain is as important as punishing the perpetrator. It's a personal decision. I will say this, though: You have one chance to gather evidence. Then it's gone. You can always collect it, then decide not to press charges.

Another important step for any survivor is to seek support. Talk to a friend, a counselor, anyone you trust that can help you navigate the next hours, weeks, and months. No one should face an assault alone.

Reporting

As a college student, you have two avenues to pursue charges. You can use your school's disciplinary system, or you can report the crime to the police (again, the standard of proof there will be higher). You could also do both. If you go to the school, they can't force you to talk to the police. They shouldn't even try. And vice versa, if you go to the police first, they won't force you to use the on-campus process.

Finding someone to talk to at school won't be hard. Every campus has a designated Title IX coordinator. Larger campuses will have multiple assistant and deputy Title IX coordinators. You can certainly seek one of them out. But my advice is to talk with the school employee you trust most. Any faculty or staff member should be able to help you. Be aware that the Title IX coordinators and most other university employees are "mandatory reporters." This means they're bound by law to report incidents even if you ask them to keep your story confidential. Every college will also have confidential resources available such as counselors, clergy, or healthcare professionals.

If you want to talk to someone confidentially, ask them before you go into any detail. Just say, "If I talk to you about a potential sexual crime on campus, are you able to keep it between you and me?" You could also outright ask, "Are you a mandatory reporter?"

SUPPORTING A FRIEND

Don't Advocate without Their Permission

Going public could be incredibly traumatic for the survivor. Publicizing details about the assault could also compromise your friend's case—both on campus and off.

Confidentially Is Key

Your friend gets to decide who else knows. Don't assume other close friends have any information.

Help Them Feel Safe

Listen to them without judgment. Don't interrogate them. Let them share at their own pace.

Take Care of Yourself

Hearing about a friend's assault can be traumatic. Keep an eye on your own mental health and seek counseling if necessary.

Some survivors immediately start poking holes in their own stories. They jump to conclusions about why the assailant won't be found guilty. Get that line of thought out of your head. If something bad happened and you want to report it—report it. Let the professionals, either at your school or in the police department, deal with everything else.

Finally, don't worry about any other rule or law you broke in relation to the assault. If you were drinking or using drugs when the incident took place, it won't matter. I guarantee you won't be charged by the police. And you won't get in trouble with the school. Both the college and the law will be focused on the assault and nothing else.

BYSTANDER INTERVENTION

Barack Obama said in his last press conference as president, "There are a lot more good people than bad in this country."[9] He was right. Those numbers work on a smaller scale too. The number of good people at any party will outnumber the bad. Bystander intervention leverages those odds. If the good people protect the vulnerable, we can prevent sexual assaults.

The idea is simple. When you see someone in distress, intercede. You can do one or more of the following:

> **Directly intervene**: Walk up and ask, "Are you okay?" or "Do you need help?"
>
> **Distract**: Create a diversion of some sort—insert yourself into the conversation, spill your drink, point to something shiny. Do whatever you can to give the target a moment to disengage and get away.
>
> **Delegate**: If the situation involves someone you don't know well, find one of their friends. Tell them, "Hey, I think your buddy is about to make a mistake" or "I think your roommate might need to be bailed out."
>
> **Delay**: If all else fails, stay nearby to keep an eye on the situation. Maybe it'll clear up on its own. Or you might think of a solution in the interim.

This may seem simple. But there's a wide gap between theories on a page and putting them into practice. You have to approach intervention the right way. A misstep could make matters worse.

Think of Your Safety Too

If you prevent a sexual assault, you're definitely a hero. But you're not a superhero. That means you could get hurt, especially if you're directly intervening. You may think you're being subtle. But the aggressor might interpret your intervention as an accusation. So be indirect. The best interventions happen without the aggressor even knowing what's going on. It could be as simple as offering a ride to the person who's in trouble. I'm sure you can think of much better schemes than I can.

One of the best male-to-male scenarios I've heard of involved a guy who saw his friend aggressively hitting on a girl at a party. They were both drunk. He knew nothing good was going to come out of the interaction. He went to his buddy, pulled him aside and said, "Hey, I don't think she's that interested in you, but there's a girl downstairs. I don't even know her name. She only knows me because I'm friends with you. She really likes you. She made me come up here to bring you to meet her. Let's go talk to her." Then he brought his friend downstairs where, of course there was no girl. She was made up. No one's feelings were hurt, and the situation was dealt with.

When to Get Involved

First, trust your instincts. You're older, smarter, and more experienced than you think you are. If your gut is telling you something isn't right, there's a good chance that's the case. Second, act sooner rather than later. It's easy to subtly get between two people when they're in a crowded room. It's a lot harder if they've gone off by themselves. There's also no real downside to jumping in too quickly. The worst that can happen is your friend says they're fine. But if you wait too long you might miss your opportunity.

BRANDON VANDENBURG

On June 22, 2013, a female student at Vanderbilt University went to a Nashville bar called the Tin Roof with a few of her friends. Court documents refer to her as E.L. She had a summer job at the athletic department and was staying on campus between semesters. She and her friends got to the bar around midnight. The guy she had been casually dating, Brandon Vandenburg, was already there when she walked in.[10]

Vandenburg was a tight end on the football team. E.L. initially met him in January when he came to campus on a recruiting visit—before that he had gone to a junior college in California. He'd only been on campus for a few weeks[11] and, according to her roommate, E.L. and Vandenburg had been "hanging out" since then.[12]

E.L. drank three ounces of gin in her apartment before leaving,[13] then had four or five drinks at the bar: a gin and tonic, a Red Bull and vodka, a shot of whiskey, and a blue mixed drink that was some kind of Long Island iced tea. She got the shot and the iced tea from Vandenburg. E.L. testified that by the time she was on her last drink she started to feel drunk. She doesn't remember if she finished it or not.[14]

E.L.'s next clear memory was waking up alone and in a lot of pain the next morning. She was in an unfamiliar room in a Vanderbilt residence hall. She was fully clothed, and her phone and keys were on the dresser next to her. She left the dorm a few hours later (after talking to a friend who lived across the hall) and found her car outside. She had no idea how she, or her car, got there. [15]

We might not know what happened that night if it wasn't for a random, unrelated act of vandalism. The same evening someone kicked in a door on the second floor of Vandenburg's residence hall. It was pulled off its hinges and cracked down the middle. A maintenance worker reported the damage to campus police who combed through security footage looking for the culprit. What they uncovered was far more insidious.

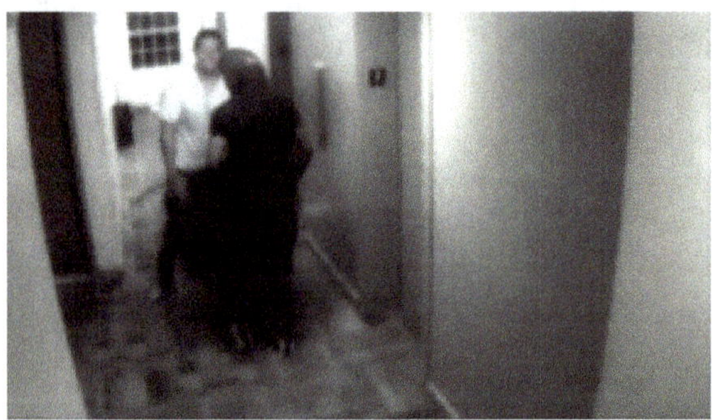

FIGURE 4.1   Vandenburg and Banks dragging E.L. through the hallway and into Vandenburg's dorm room.

First, they saw Vandenburg and three of his teammates, Tip McKenzie, Corey Batey, and Brandon Banks, carry E.L.'s limp, unconscious body out of a car and into the dorm. On the second floor, Vandenburg and Banks dragged her out of the elevator and dumped her body in the middle of the hallway. They paused for a moment to take pictures of her, then carried her into Vandenburg's room. Thirty minutes later, Vandenburg came back into the hallway, half dressed. He had a towel over his face and threw a second towel over the camera. The footage was given to the Nashville Police Department, who opened an investigation.[16] A horrifying picture of what happened that night emerged.

Apparently Vandenburg and E.L. initially went to her apartment after leaving the Tin Roof, but they couldn't get in. She'd misplaced her keys, so Vandenburg drove her car back to his dorm. He met Banks, Batey, and McKenzie outside. By this time E.L. had passed out. The four of them carried her up to Vandenburg's room[17] and sexually assaulted her. She was completely unconscious the entire time. Vandenburg handed out condoms and encouraged the others to rape E.L. Batey penetrated her vaginally and orally with his finger and penis. At one point Batey penetrated her anus with a water bottle. He also urinated on E.L. and sat on her face. Vandenburg attempted to penetrate E.L. but couldn't get an erection. Instead, he took photos and videos of the assault and sent them to friends around campus and beyond.[18] I could go into more harrowing detail. But I think the point's been made.

Banks, Batey, McKenzie, and Vandenburg were all charged with aggravated rape and sexual battery. Vandenburg was also charged with a count of unlawful photography. A few other students who helped cover up evidence the next day were charged as accessories after the fact. Everyone either pled or was found guilty. McKenzie, who cooperated with the investigation, got 10 years of probation. Batey and Banks were sentenced to 15 years in prison. Vandenburg will serve 17.[19]

FIGURE 4.2   Brandon Vandenburg in court.

That anyone would take advantage of an unconscious woman, let alone their girlfriend, in this way is unthinkable. It's hard to have much faith in humanity after hearing even the rough outline of what happened that night. There's also a lot that can be learned. The first, and most obvious point, is that there are some truly, undeniably evil people like Brandon Vandenburg in the world.

But I don't want you to focus on Vandenburg or his teammates. I want you to think about the people near the story. The ones who could have stepped in and prevented this. How many people at the bar noticed E.L.'s condition? She went there with a group of her friends. Where were they?

The security footage shows others nearby at multiple points. When the four teammates were pulling an unconscious body out of the car in front of the dorm, a female student passed by. She must've known someone involved, because she chatted with them for a few seconds then left. There was another male student in the lobby when they carried E.L. through. A few minutes later, when they were dragging E.L. down the hallway toward Brandon's room, someone got off the elevator with takeout food, then simply walked on.

FIGURE 4.3   A student coming out of the elevator while E.L. is dragged into a room and a young woman walking by as E.L. is being pulled out of her car.

Any one of those three could have called campus police. The student on the elevator could have even told them which room to check.

Also, Vandenburg's roommate was in the room during the assault. He says he woke up and saw E.L. lying face down on the bed, unconscious, with the four men around her. He heard the assailants talking about having sex with her. Instead of doing anything, he feigned sleep until it was over, then left.[20]

How many other people—in the bar, while she was being moved around town, or dragged through the dorm—saw E.L. in distress? There were surely dozens. If just one of them had done the right thing this horrible crime might have been prevented.

During your time at school, you might see someone being taken advantage of. You'll have a choice to make. You could look the other away. You could, God forbid, participate like Banks, Batey and Mackenzie did. Or you could do the right thing and get in the way. Protect whoever's in trouble and stop the assault dead in its tracks. That's bystander intervention. And that's what I want you think about as you finish this section.

CHAPTER SUMMARY

Title IX is the law that guarantees equal treatment, regardless of gender, in education. It applies to every facet of the college experience, including academics, extracurricular activities, and athletics. Colleges also need to maintain a learning environment free of harassment, discrimination, and sexual assaults.

All sexual assault statutes and policies have consent at their core. Without consent, sexual contact is an assault. Most sexual assault cases adjudicated on college campuses involve a lack of consent due to incapacitation. Usually it's due to alcohol consumption, but sometimes drugs. There's no bright line rule to determine how much alcohol is too much. In an on-campus hearing it will be determined on a case-by-case basis.

Students who have been assaulted can report the crime to either the school or the police. On campus they can talk to a designated Title IX coordinator or any staff member they trust. The coordinators and most other university employees are "mandatory reporters," meaning they're required to notify the school of a potential assault, even if the survivor wishes for the information to remain confidential. Most schools have confidential resources such as counseling services or clergy.

Bystander intervention is one of the best ways students can protect one another from sexual assaults. If you see someone in a potentially harmful situation you should take action to diffuse the situation. You can directly intervene, distract the parties, delegate to someone else, or delay. Be sure to think about your safety when intervening.

NOTES

1   Education Amendments of 1972, Title IX, 20 U.S.C. §1681-§1688 (1972).
2   Andrew, Lisa. "Michigan, Alabama and 23 More of the Most Expensive College Football Programs." *Yahoo! Finance*, 31 December 2021, https://

finance.yahoo.com/news/michigan-alabama-23-more-most-130140434.
html. Accessed 10 October 2022.

3   TX Penal Code § 22.011 (2021).

4   Ibid.

5   MN Stat § 609.344 (2021).

6   "Definitions." *University of Vermont Office of Compliance Services.
Discrimination, Harassment, and Sexual Misconduct, Definitions,
https://www.uvm.edu/sites/default/files/UVM-Policies/policies/
sexharass.pdf. Accessed 15 October 2022.

7   Ibid.

8   Negrusz, Adam., et al. "Estimate of the Incidence of Drug-Facilitated
Sexual Assault in the U.S." *U.S. Department of Justice, Office of Justice
Programs*, 2005.

9   "Obama's Last News Conference: Full Transcript and Video." *New
York Times*, 18 January 2018, https://www.nytimes.com/2017/01/18/
us/politics/obama-final-press-conference.html.

10   Luther, Jessica. "A look at Complex Vanderbilt Rape Case That
Left a Community Reeling." *Sports Illustrated*, 9 February 2015,
https://www.si.com/college/2015/02/09/vanderbilt-rape-case-bran-
don-vandenburg-cory-batey.

11   Ibid.

12   Tennessee v. Brandon Vandenburg, No. M2017-01882-CCA-R3-CD.
Opinion, p. 22 (Tenn. Ct. App.) (2019).

13   Ibid.

14   Ibid.

15   Ibid.

16   Luther, "A look at Complex Vanderbilt Rape Case."

17   Tennessee v. Brandon Vandenburg.

18   Ibid.

19   Associated Press. "Fourth Former Vanderbilt Player Gets Probation
in Rape." *Washington Post*, 21 May 2018.

20   Tennessee v. Brandon Vandenburg.

Credits

Fig. 4.1: Source: https://abcnews.go.com/WNT/video/football-player
-vanderbilt-rape-trial-sentenced-15-25-40003276.

Fig. 4.2: Source: https://www.youtube.com/watch?v=mnYXL5pl_t8.

Fig. 4.3a: Source: https://abcnews.go.com/2020/video/video-shows-van-
derbilt-football-player-carrying-date-dorm-32067934.

Fig. 4.3b: Source: https://abcnews.go.com/2020/video/video-shows-van-
derbilt-football-player-carrying-date-dorm-32067934.

PART III

TECHNOLOGY

Here's a simple rule of thumb for avoiding trouble with technology: If you wouldn't do it offline, don't do it online. Stick to this and you'll be in the clear.

It's amazing how often students make digital moves they'd never consider in the real world. Consider one of the most common mistakes—posting pictures of underage drinking. The urge is understandable. You're having an epic Thursday night and your phone is filling up with shots of the partying. You want your friends to see how much fun you're having.

Now apply the offline-equivalent test: Would anyone in their right mind print out hundreds of poster-sized pictures of themselves breaking the law, then tape them up all over campus? Of course not. But when you post self-incriminating pictures, that's exactly what you're doing—except the reach of digital publication is much wider. When you post a picture online you've essentially distributed an infinite number of copies across the entire world. And if someone did plaster the student union with a bunch of physical, criminal snapshots, they'd expect to be punished. But when students are caught online, they're absolutely flabbergasted.

We change our behaviors, our expectations, and our ethics when we engage with technology. People who would never steal a DVD from a bin at Walmart stream pirated movies without a thought. Students who wouldn't dare peek at their neighbor's answers during an exam cut and paste from the internet with abandon. Guys who couldn't imagine flashing women from a dark alley unthinkingly send unsolicited genital pics. Avoid these kinds of pitfalls. Before you do anything questionable with your tech, identify the real-world equivalent. If you wouldn't do it in person, don't use your iPhone to do the same thing digitally.

SEX AND TECHNOLOGY

PHOTOGRAPHIC SEXTING

The latest large-scale survey of high schoolers showed that one in five had texted a naked picture of themselves to someone else. Just over a quarter had received one.[1] Given that 38% of high schoolers report having sex[2] and 84% have smartphones[3], it doesn't quite add up that only a fifth have shared nudes. I suspect dishonest respondents somewhere in this mix.

The older people get, the more they sext. The most recent study that measured college students and sexting put the number at around 70%.[4] And a 2015 survey found that 88% of adults had sent naked pictures to one another.[5] I'd rather not think about how this data trend applies to retirement communities.

Above a certain age, then, most of us are sexting. And there's nothing inherently wrong with, or illegal about, two consenting adults sending naked snapshots to one another. The key words being consenting and adults. Problems arise when either of those two conditions aren't met.

The Critical Threshold: 18 Years Old

Under federal and state laws any video or picture of a person under 18 engaging in sexually explicit conduct is child pornography. College students, unfortunately, land right around that over/under line. Most first-year students are at least 18. Still, every college student has at least a few friends, maybe even a significant other, who are 17 or younger.

Federal law prohibits the possession, the distribution, and the manufacture of child pornography. Each is dealt with in a separate statute. Read through the three laws to see how they're constructed:

Federal Statute—Possession

Any person who—

(B) knowingly possesses, or knowingly accesses with intent to view, 1 or more books, magazines, periodicals, films, video tapes, or other matter which contain any visual depiction that has been mailed, or has been shipped or transported using any means or facility of interstate or foreign commerce or in or affecting interstate or foreign commerce, or which was produced using materials which have been mailed or so shipped or transported, by any means including by computer, if—

    (i) the producing of such visual depiction involves the use of a minor engaging in sexually explicit conduct; and

    (ii) such visual depiction is of such conduct;

       shall be punished as provided in subsection (b) of this section.[6]

Federal Statute—Distribution

(a) Any person who—

    (1) knowingly transports or ships using any means or facility of interstate or foreign commerce or in or affecting interstate or foreign commerce by any means including by computer or mails, any visual depiction, if—

        (A) the producing of such visual depiction involves the use of a minor engaging in sexually explicit conduct; and

        (B) such visual depiction is of such conduct;

           shall be punished as provided in subsection (b) of this section.[7]

Federal Statute—Manufacture

(a) Any person who employs, uses, persuades, induces, entices, or coerces any minor to engage in, or who has a minor assist any other person to engage in, or who transports any minor in or affecting interstate or foreign commerce, or in any Territory or Possession of the United States, with the intent that such

> minor engage in, any sexually explicit conduct for
> the purpose of producing any visual depiction of
> such conduct or for the purpose of transmitting a
> live visual depiction of such conduct, shall be pun-
> ished as provided under subsection (e)[.][8]

Know that "sexually explicit" doesn't require actual sexual activity. Nudity alone qualifies. The federal penalties for a first offense of possession or distribution are 10 years in prison if the child depicted is over 12, 20 years if the child is 11 or younger, plus fines and time on the sex offense registry. Penalties for manufacture are 5 to 20 years in prison, plus fines and inclusion on the sex offense registry for the first offense.

States also have their own child pornography laws. Although the wording varies, they all operate similarly to the federal statutes.

> Iowa's possession statute states the following:

> It shall be unlawful to knowingly purchase or possess
> a visual depiction of a minor engaging in a prohibited
> sexual act or the simulation of a prohibited sexual act.[9]

> North Carolina's Distribution law includes this:

> (a) Offense. – A person commits the offense of second
>   degree sexual exploitation of a minor if, knowing the
>   character or content of the material, he:
> (2) Distributes, transports, exhibits, receives, sells, pur-
>   chases, exchanges, or solicits material that contains
>   a visual representation of a minor engaged in sexual
>   activity.[10]

Washington state's statute about the manufacture of child pornography says:

> (1) A person is guilty of sexual exploitation of a minor
>   if the person:
> (b) Aids, invites, employs, authorizes, or causes a
>   minor to engage in sexually explicit conduct,
>   knowing that such conduct will be photo-
>   graphed or part of a live performance;[11]

As in the federal law, the definitions of "sexually explicit" or "sexual activity" are broad under state laws. Simple nudity would qualify. This means that a 15-year-old girl who sends a topless picture of herself to a guy she likes could be charged with the manufacture, distribution, and possession of child pornography—potentially under both state and federal law. And her crush could be charged with possession for simply getting the text and looking at it.

But the black letter of the law and what happens in court are two very different things. Our system allows judges and prosecutors to adjust in order to avoid unwarranted outcomes—like an adolescent girl serving 20 years for sexting. Looking at the outcomes in a few specific cases, then, is the best way to explore this topic. Since the critical delineation is 18 years old, we'll go through an example in each of three categories: everyone under 18, one person over and one under, and everyone over 18.

Everyone Under 18

Even the earliest sexting prosecutions resulted in misdemeanor convictions or less when all the participants were minors. One of the first took place in Greensburg, Pennsylvania, in 2009. Three girls from the middle school, all 14 and 15 years old, texted nudes to their boyfriends. One of the boys was caught using his phone during school hours, and it was confiscated. That's when the authorities found the naked pictures.

FIGURE 5.1   The middle school in Greensburg, PA, where students were charged with child pornography violations for sexting in 2009.

The police charged the girls with all three crimes under PA statutes—the manufacture, distribution, and possession of child pornography. The boys, who were 16 and 17 years old, were charged with possession.[12] If convicted, the girls could have faced 20 years in prison. The boys 5. There would have also been sex offense registration and steep fines for them all. Thankfully, cooler heads prevailed. The case was settled before it went to trial. All six teens pled down to misdemeanors and were sentenced to community service and curfews.[13]

In the nascent days of sexting this was a common pattern: Minors who were caught sexting would be charged under their state's child pornography laws. Then prosecutors would work out a plea deal that lessened the penalties to something much more fitting than decades in prison. Over the last 10 years many states have carved out exceptions to child pornography laws for minor-only incidents, essentially codifying what the judicial system has done from the start. Pennsylvania changed their law in 2013. Now if two minors (over 12) share sexts consensually it's a summary offense (like a traffic ticket).[14] Other states have made similar changes. New Mexico amended its child pornography law to include the following:

> B. The provisions of Subsection A of this section shall not apply to a depiction possessed by a child under the age of eighteen in which the depicted child is between the ages of fourteen and eighteen and the depicted child knowingly and voluntarily consented to the possession, and;
>
> (1) the depicted child knowingly and voluntarily consented to the creation of the depiction; or
>
> (2) the depicted child knowingly and voluntarily produced the depiction without coercion.[15]

The bottom line is this: If everyone involved is under 18 and no one was coerced, the authorities will likely be lenient. This is true even in states in which the laws haven't been amended. It may take some negotiation, but the penalties will be in line with a misdemeanor. That's not to say that the process won't have serious consequences. It will be trying on many fronts. Still, the risk of spending time in prison is extremely low.

One Over and One Under 18

This is the danger zone. An adult who sexts a minor could face low-level legal penalties. They could be charged with corruption of minors or the dissemination of harmful materials to children. In Texas, for example, selling, distributing, or exhibiting "harmful material" to anyone under 18 is a class A misdemeanor.[16] The federal statute prohibits giving "obscene materials" to juveniles under 16.[17] There are similar laws in every state. They're classified as either high-level misdemeanors or low-level felonies.

The inverse situation—when a minor sends an adult a sext—is where the most serious legal jeopardy lies. This can be the case even if the age of consent is lower than 18. In other words, in many states it's legal to have sex with someone but illegal to possess a naked picture of that same person.

The 2016 case of a Philadelphia resident illustrates this well. There, a 25-year-old man had a consensual relationship with a freshman woman at Eastern University, a local Christian school. It started when she was 16 and he was 24 and lasted roughly a year and a half. As many couples do, they sexted one another, and he recorded them having sex with his phone (with her permission).

At some point the girl's mother found out about the relationship— and the pictures—and complained to the police. The man turned himself in and admitted to possessing the videos and sexts. The police found four videos of him having sex with the girl and 79 explicit photos of her on his phone. He was charged with the following:

→ Eighty-three counts of possession of child pornography
→ Eighty-three counts of criminal use of a communications facility
→ Four counts of corruption of a minor
→ Four counts of depiction of a sexual act with a minor on a computer

If convicted, he could have been sentenced to 170 years in jail.[18]

IF SOMEONE UNDERAGE SEXTS YOU

First, delete the picture—immediately.
Then send a text back stating the following:
1. You never asked the sender to sext you
2. That you immediately deleted what they sent
3. That you don't want them to sext you again

Save the text to show it to the authorities later on if you need to.

Think about how the laws worked here. It was legal for him to have sex with this young woman. The Pennsylvania statutory rape law makes it illegal for someone to have "sexual intercourse with a complainant to whom the person is not married who is under the age of 16 years."[19] But having sexually explicit videos and pictures of her on his phone was child pornography.

He ended up pleading guilty to a single charge of corruption of minors. He was sentenced to five years' probation and ordered to have no further contact with the girl. He even got his phone back after the evidence was removed.[20] That may seem like a good outcome. And, in many respects, it was. But he does have a conviction on his record—involving sexual images of a minor. And going forward, if a potential employer Googles him, a headline about being charged with 200 counts of child pornography will inevitably come up.

The case of a 24-year-old sexting with a 16-year-old may seem far removed from the average college student. Don't let the large age gap in the Philadelphia case cloud your perception. The law would have applied in exactly the same way had a 17-year-old freshman been sexting and sleeping with an 18-year-old.

Everyone Over 18

If both parties are willing, there's nothing illegal about two adults sexting one another. Still, there are acts that can get you into serious trouble. The most common is distributing sexts without the sender's permission.

Nonconsensual Distribution of Sexts

Sext sharing is incredibly common. In a 2016 survey, roughly a quarter of college students admitted to distributing sexts they received without permission. On average, they said they sent the picture to three or more friends. Three quarters of the people in the same study said that they worried that their sexts might be shared.[21] Their fears were apparently justified.

Almost every state in the nation has a law that explicitly prohibits sharing intimate pictures without permission. South Carolina and Massachusetts are the last holdouts. California was the first state to pass a nonconsensual dissemination law. A violation there carries a sentence of up to six months in prison and a fine of up to $1000:

A person who intentionally distributes the image of the intimate body part or parts of another identifiable person, or an image of the person depicted engaged in an act of sexual intercourse, sodomy, oral copulation, sexual penetration, or an image of masturbation by the person depicted or in which the person depicted participates, under circumstances in which the persons agree or understand that the image shall remain private, the person distributing the image knows or should know that distribution of the image will cause serious emotional distress, and the person depicted suffers that distress.[22]

The statute refers to an "identifiable person" in the first sentence. You might think that means that a face or other unique feature needs to be visible in the image. The standard is much lower. Courts have held that if anyone, including the subject, can tell who's in the picture, they're identifiable for the purposes of the law.[23]

Note that the law doesn't require an explicit agreement. It applies when those involved "understand that the image shall remain private" or when the person depicted suffers emotional distress from the distribution. That covers almost every sext ever sent. Unless a picture comes with a note that says, "Show this to whoever you want; I don't care," distribution is likely illegal.

DON'T TRUST TECHNOLOGICAL SAFEGUARDS

Any claim that an app can prevent a picture from being copied or forwarded is a lie. There's always a workaround. If you want something, like a sext, to stay private, you're going to have to ensure its safekeeping. Technology will never do that job for you.

These laws are a meaningful step toward stopping the unauthorized distribution of sexts. But in practical terms they won't do much to protect victims. Conviction rates are low, even in the most aggressive jurisdictions. And even if a perpetrator is found guilty, the fines and jail sentences imposed won't solve the real problem. The intimate images will stay in circulation no matter how severely the offender is punished. The justice system is useful for solving certain kinds of problems. This isn't one of them. Laws and punishments can't erase intimate pictures from the dark corners of the internet once they've been leaked.

Nonconsensual Sexts

Sexting without an invitation, or even warning, is largely a male-to-female problem. And it's a big one. A 2020 survey showed that 44% of American women had received an unsolicited picture of a male member.[24] Astounding. A 2017 survey from the United Kingdom found about the same. Forty one percent of British women said they'd received an unexpected groin portrait. But, more interestingly, only 5% percent of the men from the same study admitted to sending an unsolicited sext.[25] Either some of the participants were lying, or 5% of the men in the UK are so incredibly proud of their penises they've sent pictures of them out to nearly half of the British female population.

Cyber-flashing has become so common that a few states have passed laws to prohibit it. Texas enacted a statute in 2019 that says a person commits an offense if the person knowingly transmits by electronic means visual material that:

> (1) depicts:
>
>> (A) any person engaging in sexual conduct or with the person's intimate parts exposed; or
>> (B) covered genitals of a male person that are in a discernibly turgid state; and
>
> (2) is not sent at the request of or with the express consent of the recipient[.][26]

It's a class C misdemeanor, punishable by a fine of up to $500. Expect more jurisdictions to enact similar laws in the near future. In states that don't have directed prohibitions against unsolicited sexting, offenders could be prosecuted under existing harassment laws.

Put legality aside for a moment. Sending a picture of your intimate parts probably won't have the desired effect. The 2020 survey also asked women how they felt about the penis pictures. Seventy percent had a negative reaction. Half reported feeling "grossed out," and 46% felt disrespected. A paltry 16% reported having anything positive to say. And even fewer, only 8%, reported feeling aroused.[27]

The reactions differed based on gender and sexual orientation. Men of all sexual identities view receiving sexts more positively than women do. Still, less than half (44%) of gay and bisexual men said they were entertained by unexpected penis cameos.[28]

Unless you're 100% sure the person you're texting wants to see a picture of your privates, don't send one. It's illegal, and it won't endear you to the recipient. How will you know they want to see your junk? They'll tell you. They'll say something along the lines of "I'd like to see a naked picture of you. Please send one." Barring that, it's best to leave the nude portraiture to Botticelli and Goya.

SEXTORTION

In the fall of 2015, a senior at Utah Valley University named Jake Curtis met a woman on Kik. She said her name was Mariz Abril. He chatted with her for a few days. He told her about his job loading trucks for UPS in the early morning hours before school and his plans to be an elementary school teacher after graduation. Jake was, according to his mother, a late bloomer and had just started dating. Eventually the woman he'd been flirting with asked for a naked photo. He obliged. Then texted back "Where's mine?"

He immediately got a message back: "Just added and saved all your Facebook friends on my laptop." Then she (although it could have been a man) threatened to send the picture to all of Jake's friends, his family, and to his bosses at UPS. "But I will not do that if you send me money right now, okay?" she messaged.

Over the next few days Jake made three wire payments to his blackmailer totaling $680—every cent he had. He sent messages explaining that he was out of money. He even sent a screenshot of his bank account showing there was nothing left. His extortionist didn't relent and kept demanding more cash. Look at the following exchange.

> Jake: I don't have any more [money].
>
> Blackmailer: You better find some.
>
> Jake: You won't get any money if I'm not around.
>
> Blackmailer: Oh, you're going to kill yourself? Like the five other guys did? I don't care, go ahead. You better find a way to get the money or you find a way to kill yourself.

Jake couldn't see a way out. Just five days after he sent the nude photo, he went to his family's vacation home and shot himself. He left behind six notes to friends and family members, all the transcripts of the online conversations, records of the wire transfers, and his iPhone—unlocked so that it could be accessed. He might have felt that his situation was beyond hope, but he seemed to want justice.

The police investigation revealed that the blackmailers were based in the Philippines. And it uncovered other victims. "Mariz Abril" had been wired nearly $30,000 from 24 men in 18 U.S. states between 2010 and 2015. But because Abril (or whoever she was) was offshore, there was little the authorities could do.[29]

The Curtis case is textbook sextortion—the threat of the distribution of intimate texts to blackmail the victim. Often the extortionists are after money. Sometimes they ask for additional, more graphic, pictures. There was even a case in Wisconsin in which a high school student coerced seven young men, aged 15 to 17, to perform sex acts on him with the threat of distributing nude pictures.[30]

Sextortion cases are increasingly common. In 2021 the FBI received more than 18,000 complaints about online extortion with losses of nearly $14 million.[31] College students need to take steps to avoid entrapment:

→ **Unless you've met them, don't sext them.**

  If you don't actually know someone, don't send them a naked picture. Sexting a stranger is literally asking for trouble.

→ **Use Google.**

  When interacting with someone online, at the very least, Google their name before revealing too much of yourself. Had Jake Curtis done a simple online search, there's a chance "Mariz Abril" would have come up as a known scammer.

→ **Trust your gut.**

  If something seems off, trust that instinct and lean into it. Chances are you're right.

→ **If you're being blackmailed, don't play the game.**

  Shut down all communication. Don't give in to their demands. And report the crime either to local police or at cybercrime.gov.

DATING APPS

Sex offenders have realized that Tinder, Grinder, and Hinge are excellent places to hunt for potential victims. No one collects official national statistics in the U.S. about online dating and sexual violence. But in 2019, Columbia Journalism Investigations and Pro Publica surveyed more than 1,200 women who had used a digital dating platform in the last 15 years. Nearly a third—31%—reported being sexually assaulted by someone they met via dating sites or apps.[32]

The companies that own these apps can't, or won't, do much to protect their users. Match Group—which owns Tinder, Match, Hinge, and 40 other online dating brands—doesn't perform criminal checks on its free platforms. They don't collect enough information from users to even know who they are. As a company spokesperson said, "There are definitely registered sex offenders on our free products."[33] Further, when assaults and rapes are reported directly to these companies, the responses are inadequate. Moderators are expected to resolve complaints in a matter of minutes. They have quotas. And the moderation teams are tiny compared to the number of users.[34]

It's not hard to find stories of women (the violence is predominantly male to female, but it does occur in all gender combinations) meeting men via a dating app, then being assaulted, raped, or even killed by their digital matches. Do a news search for "dating app assault" and dozens will come up. One of the more harrowing, and instructive, is that of Shane Steven Allen.

In 2016 Allen met a 20-year-old University of Kansas student on Tinder. He picked her up at her sorority house on April 12 and brought her to the trailer he lived in. Two of Allen's friends, both men, came over that evening and hung out with Allen and his date for a few hours. After they left, Allen flew into a jealous rage, accusing the woman of flirting with one of them. He punched her. Then, after she fell to the ground, kept kicking and beating her for a half hour.

After the initial assault ended, she pleaded with him to take her back to campus. He refused. He said he couldn't let her leave until the swelling around her eyes went down; otherwise, he might get into trouble. For the next six days Allen held her hostage, periodically beating her and choking her. He also forced her to contact her friends to assure them that she was okay. Finally, after she promised not to go to the authorities, Allen relented and took her back to campus. She arrived with two black eyes; bruises and swelling on her head, face, and neck;

and abrasions all over her body. Allen was arrested and charged with one felony count of kidnapping and four felony counts of battery.[35]

That, in and of itself, is a horrifying story. Sadly, it's only the first part. In return for pleading no contest to two counts of battery, Allen was granted probation. As a condition of his release, he was ordered to stay off all dating sites and apps. But two years later he connected with a 27-year-old woman named Sabrina Frock on Meetme.com. She drove herself to his trailer on a Wednesday night in late April 2018. Two days later Allen called 911. When the EMTs got there, Frock was unconscious from a severe head injury. She was flown to the University of Kansas Hospital where she underwent brain surgery. She never regained consciousness and died on May 1.[36]

Her death was ruled suspicious, but due to a lack of evidence (Allen is the only living witness and claims her death was accidental), he hasn't been charged.[37] We may never definitively know what happened to Sabrina Frock.

Think about the circumstances that led Frock to the trailer where, just two years prior, Allen held a Tinder date hostage for six days. Certainly, the justice system didn't work well. Allen shouldn't have been released in the first place.

For me, though, the main takeaway is that dating app companies have little ability, and no real motivation, to safeguard their users. It's far too easy for someone with a criminal background—or even a sexual assault conviction—to create an account. That means the burden falls on you, the user, to protect yourself.

DATING APP SAFETY TIPS

Stick to Paid Apps

A service you pay for is much more likely to actually screen users against criminal databases.

Control the Situation

If you can, stay in control by being the one who chooses the venue for early in-person meetings. Choose a neutral, public location.

Give as Little Personal Information as Possible Early On

It's fine to bond and share. That's what you're there for. But leave identifying details out. For example, say that you're going to school, not that you're attending a specific college.

Stay Anonymous to Start

Keep your contact information private until you're ready to meet in person. You want to be able to cleanly disengage if you decide you're not interested. In the early stages communicate through the app or another anonymous service like Google Voice.

Confirm Identities before a Date

Change that strategy if you decide you actually want to get together with your match. Switch to something that will allow you to verify their identity. Swap a few snaps on Snapchat or have a video call to make sure they are who they say they are.

Don't Rely on Your Date for Transportation

Either drive yourself or use a rideshare service. You need to be in control so you can leave whenever you want.

Tell a Friend

Always let someone you trust know where you're going, who you're meeting, and when you plan to be back. Tell them to assume something went wrong if you don't check in by a certain time. Let them track your phone during the date. Consider designating a code word or phrase to use if you're in trouble but can't talk openly.

CHAPTER SUMMARY

Technically, photographic sexts of minors are child pornography. Sexts between minors are generally treated leniently by the court system. When a minor sexts someone over 18 there's the potential for serious legal consequences. Adults who possess nude pictures of minors are regularly charged under child pornography laws. This is the case even in states where the age of consent (the age at which it's legal to have sex) is lower than 18. In some jurisdictions it may be legal to have sex with someone but illegal to possess a nude picture of that same person.

It is, of course, legal for two adults to sext one another. Still, there are potential dangers to avoid. The unauthorized distribution of sexts is the most common. Forty-eight states and the District of Columbia have laws that prohibit sharing a nude photo without the original sender's permission. Sending explicit pictures without permission, or warning, is also surprisingly common. It's become so prevalent that states have passed laws prohibiting nonconsensual sexts. Sextortion, blackmail with the threat of the distribution of intimate images, is also on the rise. The FBI received 18,000 complaints about online extortion in 2021.

A 2019 survey found that 31% of women who had used a digital dating platform had been assaulted by one of their digital matches. The companies that own dating apps and sites aren't able, or willing to, protect their users. They rarely do criminal checks. And, when assaults are directly reported to them, their responses are inadequate. As a spokesman for the Match Group said, "There are definitely registered sex offenders on our free products."[38] Since these companies don't protect users, college students need to take steps to ensure their own safety if they use Match, Tinder, or any other dating app.

NOTES

1   Madigan, Sheri, et al. "Prevalence of Multiple Forms of Sexting Behavior among Youth." *JAMA Pediatrics*, vol. 172, no. 4, p. 327. https://doi.org/10.1001/jamapediatrics.2017.5314.

2   "2019 Youth Risk Behavior Survey Results." Centers for Disease Control and Prevention, 2019, https://nccd.cdc.gov/Youthonline/App/Results.aspx.

3   Rideout, Vicky, and M. B. Robb. *The Common Sense Census: Media Use by Tweens and Teens.* Common Sense Media, 2019.

4   Ingram, Lucy, et al. "Sexual Behaviors, Mobile Technology Use, and Sexting Among College Students in the American South." *American Journal of Health Promotion*, vol. 33, no. 1, 2019, pp. 87-96.

5   Stasko, Emily, and Pamela Geller. "Reframing Sexting as a Positive Relationship Behavior." *Drexel University, Department of Psychology*, 2015.

6   18 U.S.C. § 2252 (2020).

7   Ibid.

8   Ibid.

9   IA Code § 728.12 (2021).

10   NC Gen Stat § 14-190.17 (2021).

11   WA Rev Code § 9.68A.040 (2021).

12   Stiles, Bob. "Federal Lawsuit Irrelevant in Greensburg Salem Sexting Case." *Pittsburgh Tribune Review*, 6 March 2009, https://archive.triblive.com/news/federal-lawsuit-irrelevant-in-greensburg-salem-sexting-case/.

13   Stephey, M. "Buzzwords Sexting." *Time*, 8 December 2009.

14   18 PA Cons Stat § 6321 (2021).

15   NM Stat § 30-6A-3 (2021).

16   TX Penal Code § 43.24 (2021).

17   18 U.S.C. §1470 (2020).

18   Rose, Alex. "It's Probation for Man Who Taped Sex with College Student." *Delaware County Daily Times*, 28 November 2016, https://www.delcotimes.com/2016/11/28/its-probation-for-man-who-taped-sex-with-college-student/.

19   8 PA Cons Stat § 3211.1 (2021).

20   Rose, "It's Probation."

21   Garcia, Justin R., et al. "Sexting among Singles in the USA: Prevalence of Sending, Receiving, and Sharing Sexual Messages and Images." *Sexual Health*, vol. 13, no. 5, 2016, p. 428. doi:10.1071/sh15240.

22   CA Penal Code § 647 (2021).

23   People v. Johnson, 234 Cal.App.4th 1432 (2015).

24   Marcotte, Alexandra S., et al. "Women's and Men's Reactions to Receiving Unsolicited Genital Images from Men." *The Journal of Sex Research*, vol. 58, no. 4, 2021, pp. 512-521. doi:10.1080/00224499.2020.1779171.

25   Manning, Ellen. "Four in Ten Millennial Women Have Been Sent an Unsolicited 'Dick Pic.' Yahoo! Sports, 16 February 2018, https://sports.yahoo.com/four-ten-millennial-women-sent-unsolicited-dick-pic-141341471.html. Accessed 10 October 2022.

26   TX Penal Code § 21.19 (2021).

27   Marcotte et al. "Women's and Men's Reactions to Receiving Unsolicited Genital Images."

28   Ibid.

29   Megas, Natalia. "Sextortion Killed Their Son. Cops Looked the Other Way. *Daily Beast*, 18 January 2018, https://www.thedailybeast.com/sextortion-killed-their-son-cops-looked-the-other-way?ref=scroll.

30   Gross, Michael Joseph. "Sextortion at Eisenhower High." *Gentlemen's Quarterly*, 30 June 2009, https://www.gq.com/story/wisconsin-high-school-sex-scandal-online-facebook.

31   "Federal Bureau of Investigation Internet Crime Report 2021." FBI, 2021, https://www.ic3.gov/Media/PDF/AnnualReport/2021_IC3Report.pdf.

32   Flynn, Hillary, et al. "Tinder Lets Known Sex Offenders Use the App. It's not the Only One." *Propublica*, 2 December 2019, https://www.propublica.org/article/tinder-lets-known-sex-offenders-use-the-app-its-not-the-only-one#methodology.

33   Ibid.

34   Edwards, Brian, et al. "Addressing Rape in Four Minutes or Less: Dating App Reps Left Unprepared to Respond to Assault Victims." ProPublica, 17 May 2021, https://www.propublica.org/article/addressing-rape-in-four-minutes-or-less-dating-app-reps-left-unprepared-to-respond-to-assault-victims. Accessed 10 October 2022.

35   Swanson, Conrad. "Lawrence Sorority Student Beaten, Kidnapped for Nearly a Week after Meeting Man on Social Media, Court Documents Allege." *Lawrence Journal-World*, 9 May 2016, https://www2.ljworld.com/news/2016/may/09/lawrence-sorority-student-held-against-her-will/.

36   Shepard, Sara. "Lawrence Police Investigating Woman's Death; Her Mother Says She Was Visiting Man Who Was Previously Convicted in Kidnapping and Beating Case." *Lawrence Journal-World*, 12 June 2018.

37   Ibid.

38   Flynn, et al. "Tinder Lets Known Sex Offenders Use the App."

Credit

SOCIAL MEDIA, CRIMES, DISCIPLINE, AND EMPLOYERS

SELFIE INCRIMINATION

Here's the simple truth: What you post can get you in trouble. Students think they're somehow protected when they fill their feeds with pictures of illegal activity. They incorrectly cite legal principles like "free speech" or "privacy" to support their assertions. They're wrong. Post something incriminating and there's a real chance it will lead to trouble—school discipline, losing your job, or even criminal charges.

The Fourth Amendment

Before we examine your constitutional right to privacy, it bears pointing out, once more, that the Bill of Rights only applies to the government. Federal and state entities must guarantee the rights included there. Private actors aren't bound by them. If you're at a public college or university, then your school is—for the most part—a state actor and must abide by constitutional constraints. Private colleges don't have to follow these rules. They can do what they want.

Still, even if you go to the most parochial school in the country, it's worth taking the time to understand the basics of digital privacy rights. And you'll see by the end of this section that, no matter which kind of school you attend, the Fourth Amendment won't do much protect you if you air your dirty laundry online.

This is the Fourth Amendment to the United States Constitution. It's the foundation of your privacy rights as a U.S. citizen:

> The right of the people to be secure in their persons, houses, papers, and effects, against unreasonable searches and seizures, shall not be violated, and no Warrants shall issue, but upon probable cause, supported by

> Oath or affirmation, and particularly describing the place
> to be searched, and the persons or things to be seized.[1]

This is the law that keeps the police from searching your house without justification. It also applies to digital information. There are still many legal gray areas that need to be defined, but two recent Supreme Court cases show that the Fourth Amendment applies to electronic data.

In *Riley v. California* (2014) the court ruled that officers can't search detainees' phone data when they perform body searches.[2] Similarly, in *Carpenter v. United States* (2018) the court held that the police need a warrant to obtain records of someone's movements generated by cell phone records.[3]

At least to some extent, then, our privacy rights extend to our personal data. But the Fourth Amendment is riddled with exceptions and caveats. The whole Bill of Rights is for that matter. On first reading, the amendments seem like bright line rules. The First Amendment says that "Congress shall make no law … abridging the freedom of speech." On its face that's a definitive statement. Same with the Second Amendment—"the right of the people to keep and bear arms, shall not be infringed."

But even the least legally minded among us knows that's not how it works. Think about free speech. You know from Chapter 1 that there are limits to your ability to express yourself. You don't have a right to possess or distribute child pornography. You can't threaten others or defame them. And even if what you're saying isn't banned speech, there are limits to how and where you can make yourself heard. The First Amendment wouldn't protect you if you interrupted classes every day. If you owned land in a residential neighborhood, zoning laws would prevent you from putting up a billboard regardless of your right to express yourself.

As for the Second Amendment, we can all think of places where guns aren't allowed—court houses, federal buildings, post offices, airports. Look around campus. There are probably dozens of signs banning firearms there too.

The Reasonable Expectation of Privacy

The Fourth Amendment functions just like the rest of the Bill of Rights. There are multiple qualifiers and exemptions. The most important caveat for online purposes is something called the reasonable expectation of privacy. This concept isn't an exception. It's a threshold that must be met. It was laid out by the Supreme Court in *Katz v. United States* (1967). There, the court said that for Fourth Amendment rights to vest, two things must be true:

1.   The person being searched must believe their property is private.
2.   That belief must be reasonable based on societal standards.[4]

Let's revisit our billboard. Assume your zoning board let you put your sign up. You're a drug dealer, so on it there's a big picture of you holding a baggie of white powder. In giant letters it says "I Love Drugs! I Love You! I'd Love to Sell You Drugs!" The ad works. Your sales go through the roof. You're happier than Heisenberg.

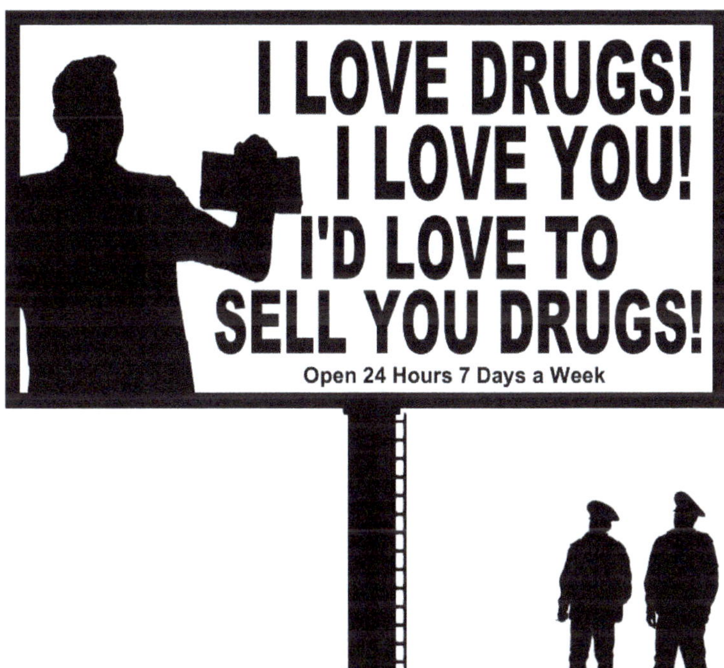

FIGURE 6.1.   "I Love Drugs!" Billboard.

What if the local police drove by and read your sign? They'd surely bring you downtown to face charges. If you said to the judge, "This isn't fair; that billboard was private. It was between me and my customers," you'd be laughed out of court. The judge would say (1) "You couldn't possibly think your statements about being a drug dealer were private—you put them on a billboard" and (2) "Even if you did, that's not a reasonable belief." In other words, you haven't passed the reasonable expectation of privacy test. The Fourth Amendment doesn't apply.

This is a strange law. It's based on what you think. And thoughts change based on what you know (or should know). Go find your school's Acceptable Use of Technology Policy. It's probably somewhere in the student handbook. There's a good chance there's a sentence or two in it that specifically nullifies the Fourth. Here's that part in the Iowa State Electronic Privacy Policy:

> Iowa State University may preserve, access, or monitor accounts and equipment during the course of an investigation of misconduct, violations of law, or violations of university policy by students or employees.[5]

Here's what the Earlham College policy says about electronic privacy when using their network:

> Under normal circumstances, College officials will not examine personal information transmitted over the network or stored on College-owned computers. However, the College reserves the right, to monitor system resources, including activity and accounts when:
>
> → necessary to protect the integrity, security, or functionality of College computing resources
>
> → an account or system is engaged in unusual or excessive activity
>
> → it has good cause to believe that the Community Principles and Practices, rules outlined in this document, or the State or Federal laws are being violated.[6]

Almost every college in the country—public or private—has some sort of language in their policies stating that they may monitor traffic and usage over the school-owned network. Some even invoke the actual legal phrase, such as this policy that covers all schools in the Connecticut State system:

7. No Expectation of Privacy

> There is no expectation of privacy in the use of CSCU IT
> resources. CSCU reserves the right to inspect, monitor
> and disclose all IT resources including files, data, pro-
> grams and electronic communications records without
> the consent of the holder of such records.[7]

It's not possible to reasonably expect that your online activity will
be private when a university policy explicitly tells you it's not. The
inclusion of these types of clauses effectively nullifies any Fourth
Amendment protections you might enjoy.

The Exclusionary Rule

But what if you're at a public college and the computer use policy
doesn't include any kind of nullifying language? Even then the Fourth
Amendment wouldn't do much to protect you on campus. Because
when the Fourth Amendment is violated, the evidence found can't
be used against you in a criminal trial. That's the only consequence.
This is called the exclusionary rule. It was laid out by the U.S. Supreme
Court in *Mapp v. Ohio* (1961).[8] If your college was going to try you in
front of a judge in an actual court, that might be useful. But that's not
what happens when you violate university policies. Your "crimes" will
be adjudicated in front of some sort of campus disciplinary board. The
exclusionary rule doesn't apply there.

Public Postings

What we've covered so far are places where you could conceivably
claim that you thought your data would stay confidential—emails,
hard drives, and maybe even cloud drives or commerce sites. When
you post content to a public platform, like Instagram or Snapchat,
you're literally putting it out there for the world to see. Even if it's only
available to a select group, like friends or followers, it isn't "private" in
the eyes of the law. Everything you put up on your feed is fair game for
both the school authorities and the police. Again, the Fourth Amendment doesn't apply.

Authentication

Students, also, often try to challenge the truth of the online evidence.
They say, "How can you prove there was vodka in that bottle? Maybe

it's just water I'm drinking?" Or, "That's not marijuana, it's a big baggie of oregano." In an actual court those arguments might work. Before evidence can be used in a real trial it has to be authenticated. The prosecutor would have to prove that the picture was truthful before it could be shown in court. The federal rules of evidence put it this way:

Rule 901. Authenticating or Identifying Evidence

> (a) In General. To satisfy the requirement of authenticating or identifying an item of evidence, the proponent must produce evidence sufficient to support a finding that the item is what the proponent claims it is.[9]

It's a somewhat complicated rule, and a full discussion of the authentication of evidence isn't necessary here. In simple terms, if a lawyer wanted to enter a post from Instagram showing you shot gunning a Budweiser as evidence that you violated underage drinking laws, she'd have to produce enough digital forensic evidence to prove the photo was authentic (hard to do) or have a witness testify that they were there when the picture was taken and that it accurately represented what happened. Otherwise, the picture couldn't be used.

But student disciplinary hearings don't have to follow the rules of evidence (see sidebar on *Nash v. Auburn University*).[10] Whatever body you're in front of—a panel of students, a dean, a coach—gets to weigh the evidence, including issues of credibility. That means anything posted online is fair game in on-campus disciplinary hearings.

NASH V. AUBURN UNIVERSITY, 1987

Two students enrolled in Auburn's Veterinary School were found guilty by the honor court of cheating on an anatomy test. They were suspended for one year. During the hearing other students and faculty testified that they had seen the accused acting suspiciously at the test in question and during prior exams. The cheaters sued the school, claiming that the on-campus hearing was unfair. Among other things, they argued that the testimony about their behavior at prior tests violated the rules of evidence and shouldn't have been discussed. The 11th Circuit Court upheld the suspensions and said, "Student disciplinary hearings follow flexible rules and need not conform to formal rules of evidence."

Standards of Proof in On-Campus Discipline

You've probably heard the term *standard of proof* before. It's the level of evidence that's necessary to establish proof of guilt in a trial. It's a sliding scale, based on the severity of the crime—or more accurately the severity of the punishment. The harsher the potential penalty, the more proof there needs to be to convict. If a guilty verdict could lead to a long prison term or an execution, the standard of proof is the highest possible level. The courts want to be absolutely sure before imposing that kind of sentence. In criminal cases, then, the juries must find "beyond a reasonable doubt" that the crime was committed by the defendant, meaning that no other plausible explanation exists for what happened.

In suits involving civil liberties the standard is "clear and convincing evidence." That roughly translates to a high probability that the allegations occurred. And in cases where only money is at stake, the standard goes down again, to a "preponderance of the evidence," which means "more likely than not."

The potential punishments a college can dole out for breaking their rules are comparatively minor. The worst they can do is expel you. Therefore, in most on-campus hearings (except for assault hearings under Title IX, which are discussed elsewhere) the standard of proof is the lowest: "more likely than not." That translates just over 50%, or better, 50% and a feather. If you're holding a can that says Budweiser on Instagram, it's more likely than not that you possessed alcohol.

Put everything contained in the previous few pages together and it becomes clear that your online privacy rights at school are almost nonexistent:

- → School officials can look at anything you post online.
- → Anything they find can be used as evidence against you in an on-campus judicial hearing.
- → One picture can be proof of an infraction.

Smart students keep photographic evidence of rule breaking off the internet.

ANONYMOUS APPS AND SITES

Every year a new confidential gossip app or site breaks onto the campus scene. In the heyday of Facebook, campus confessions pages were all the rage. From 2007 to 2009 JuicyCampus was ubiquitous—it flamed out quickly amid lawsuits and, apparently, an inability to turn a profit.[11] About a decade ago Yik Yak was omnipresent at colleges across the country. It shut down in 2017 then reappeared in the summer of 2021. There have been many other pretenders to the confidential gossip throne: Jodel, Barstool Sports, and Librex are just a few.

Most anonymous posts are innocuous. A group at MIT analyzed the content of Yik Yak in 2015 and found that roughly 95% of the chatter was mundane: discussions of parties, parking options, and other day-to-day concerns. There were also some upsides. Under the veil of anonymity users could broach taboo subjects they might not have felt comfortable bringing up elsewhere. The other 5%, though, was truly troubling. It included racist and homophobic comments, rumor slinging, and threats.[12]

De-Individuation and Dishonesty

When you think about the psychological forces at play, it makes sense that there's a dark side to apps like Yik Yak. Group dynamics, anonymity, and a lack of accountability all nudge users of anonymous apps toward bad behaviors. Ed Diener's 1976 trick or treating experiment illustrates this perfectly. That Halloween he and his colleagues put a bowl of candy on a table in the entryway of a house. About 2 feet away was a bowl of pennies and nickels. When costumed kids came in, a woman greeted them. Sometimes she asked their names and sometimes she let them remain anonymous. In some cases, she'd also tell one of the children that "they were in charge" of making sure the other kids didn't steal. She told all the trick or treaters to take one piece of candy each. Finally, she'd leave the room and covertly watch what they did.

Children who were alone and identified were the least likely to steal. Only 7.5% took extra candy. Anonymous kids in a group were much more likely to be dishonest. Almost 60% took extra candy or money. The worst offenders were the anonymous trick or treaters who knew that another child in the room was "in charge." Eighty percent stole money and/or candy. Apparently, they felt doubly insulated from repercussions. Their anonymity shielded them. And even if they did get caught, what they did was someone else's problem.[13]

Apply the findings of the Diener experiment to the average online troll. That last situation—unidentifiable and inculpable—describes anonymous apps like Yik Yak to a T. By definition, no one's identifiable.

And the site's moderators are the "kids in charge" who let everyone else off the hook.

CommuniTree, Lanker-Simons, and Shim

The structure of online communities has encouraged these base impulses since the earliest days of the internet. In the late 1970s a group of academics started an online platform called CommuniTree. Its founders wanted to create a digital salon where free speech and confidentiality were valued above all; there were few moderators, and the programming itself made it hard to ban users or remove comments. They hoped CommuniTree would become a digital forum where intellectuals from around the world could connect. For a few months that's exactly what it was.

At the same time middle and high schools started to install computer rooms for their students, often with modem access. It didn't take long for thousands of adolescent boys to find CommuniTree. They quickly filled the discussion boards with the kinds of comments you'd expect from 14-year-olds—not a lot of Dostoyevsky but plenty of dookie jokes. Eventually the sheer volume of obscenity jammed the servers, and CommuniTree was shut down. As one of the early users put it "the barbarian hordes mowed us down."[14]

There are much more recent examples of anonymity leading to bad behavior online. In 2013 the University of Wyoming campus was swept up in a controversy about a post on their UW Crushes Facebook group. The page was mostly filled with benign amorous confessions like "I think that blonde in my freshman comp class is so sexy." In early April, though, someone posted a threat of sexual violence:

> I want to hatefuck Meg Lanker-Simons so hard. That chick runs her liberal mouth all the time and doesn't care who knows it. I think it's hot and it makes me angry. One night with me and she's going to be a good republican bitch.

Lanker-Simons was, at the time, a UW student and a well-known liberal blogger. She responded to the post personally when others demanded the threat be removed, stating that she wanted it to stay up. She criticized the admins of the page for allowing it to be published and encouraged the author to seek counseling.

The situation spawned a feverish campus-wide reaction. Lanker-Simons's supporters staged a rally protesting rape culture and sexual violence. The university police investigated the threat and quickly determined that Lanker-Simons herself authored it. She initially denied the accusation.[15] But when confronted with digital evidence that implicated her, she pled no contest to misdemeanor interference with an investigation and was fined $540.[16]

It's easy to harshly judge Lanker-Simons. I choose to think that her heart was in the right place. Exploiting an anonymous Facebook page—a sleazy one at that—to draw attention to a serious cause probably made sense to her at the time. Then the situation spun out of control. Anonymity can lead to reckless decision making, even when intentions are good.

When intentions are bad things get worse. Take the case of Jong Shim at Penn State. On Saturday, October 11, 2014, he posted on Yik Yak saying that he was going to shoot everyone in the student union the following Monday. It was quickly taken down, but the police had already seen it.

Less than 12 hours later Shim, a sophomore, was arrested at his off-campus apartment. There were no weapons at his home. He told the authorities it was a just prank. He later pled guilty to one count of terroristic threats and a count of disorderly conduct. He was sentenced to serve 5 days to 12 months in jail and a year of probation. [17]

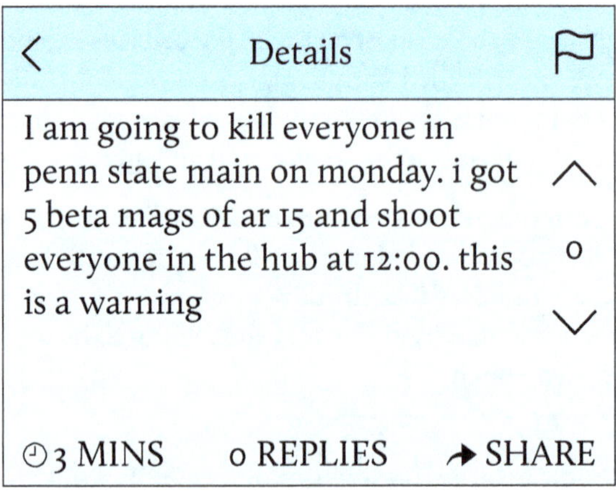

FIGURE 6.2   Jong Shim's Yik Yak post.

In a case of history (and stupidity) repeating itself, another Penn State student named Henry Hyduke pulled a nearly identical "prank" on August 24, 2022. His Yik Yak post said "ROTC bombing downtown state college tonight. Stay safe." He was also identified and arrested by police within hours.[18]

There's plenty to unpack in these cases. For starters, how could anyone think that the threat of a mass shooting or bombing is funny? But two main points stand out to me. The first is how quickly the veil of anonymity can be pierced by the authorities. There's almost always some kind of digital fingerprint left behind when you engage online. If the stakes are high enough, that data will be used to find you.

In Lanker-Simons's case, the posts to UW Crushes went through a third-party app called Survey Monkey. The police served a warrant to that company and were given the IP address, the wireless Mac address, and the username of the poster of the threat. The IP address was assigned to a computer named "ELComputerdeMeg" and the Survey Monkey username was "Meghanm." Those both matched the data on Lanker-Simons's laptop.[19] To find Shim, police reached out directly to Yik Yak who, given the imminent threat of violence, immediately handed over the GPS data for the threatening post.[20] Yik Yak is a location-based app. Messages are broadcasted only to users within a 1.5-mile radius. That means there's an exact GPS location and a correlating IP address for every yak.

The second concept I want you to take away from these stories recalls Diener and his trick-or-treaters: Anonymous online communities encourage chaos. A perception of confidentiality combined with group mentality will inevitably lead to dishonest, and sometimes dangerous, behavior. Yes, there are upsides to anonymity. And gossip can be endlessly entertaining. But, at the very least, think about what you're getting into before you wade into these dangerous digital waters.

EMPLOYERS AND SOCIAL MEDIA

In a 2020 poll, 67% of hiring managers said they regularly used social networking sites to research candidates. More than half said they'd eliminated a candidate because of what they found.[21] A 2018 survey asked hiring managers about the kinds of online content that led them to reject applicants. Their answers ran the gamut from provocative or inappropriate images (40%), to drinking or drug use (38%), racist comments (31%), poor communication skills (27%), and even that the candidate talked badly about a previous employer (25%).[22]

Again, think of the offline equivalent of your online actions. Posting party pics when you're job hunting is like printing 8 × 10 glossies of yourself in compromising situations and showing them to the head of HR during your interview. Assume everything you put online will be seen by someone who is deciding whether to hire you—now and potentially in the future.

Consider Alexi McCammond. She was one of print media's rising stars. She was named the 2019 emerging journalist of the year by the National Association of Black Journalists.[23] In the Spring of 2021, at 27, she was named the Editor in Chief of Teen Vogue. Shortly after Condé Nast announced her appointment, offensive tweets she posted in 2011 resurfaced. The half dozen posts were mostly anti-Asian, and a few contained homophobic slurs. A picture of her in a Native American costume at a Halloween party also came to light at the same time.

The company had been aware of the anti-Asian tweets (but not the other offensive posts). McCammond deleted those in 2019 and issued a public apology. And she acknowledged them in interviews for the job. Condé Nast decided to hire her despite that digital past, thinking she had learned from her mistakes, which was surely true. Still, when McCammond's appointment was announced, employees of *Teen Vogue* publicly complained, which drew widespread attention in the media. Two weeks after being offered the job she was forced to withdraw.[24]

 Alexi McCammond on MSNBC in 2019.

Think about what happened here: McCammond lost a job because of tweets that were 10 years old. At 27 she was punished for the actions of her 17-year-old self. Further, some of the posts that surfaced—the homophobic slurs and the insensitive costume—reappeared long after she took them down. Presumably one of her friends or followers had saved them, then shared them after her promotion was announced.

Aside from the obvious lesson—that racist tweets will get you fired—there are two main takeaways. First, cancellation doesn't have a statute of limitations. What you post today could conceivably resurface decades from now and cause serious trouble. Second, it's nearly impossible to delete something once it's been published digitally. The internet has a long and judgmental memory. When you post you relinquish all control. You can't know who's saved something or when it might show up again.

GETTING A JOB

Clean Up your Username

No one is going to hire you if your handle is @tokeallday or @pornaddict.

Don't Bad Mouth Current or Future Employers

Avoid criticisms of your employer or any company you might want to work for in the future.

Watch Strong Political or Religious Posts

Having deeply held beliefs is a good thing. Still, you don't want a potential employer to make a snap judgment based on your views.

Don't Be Stupid or Racist (Same Thing)

Pictures of you breaking the law or that are racist will keep you from getting a job.

YOUR DIGITAL IMAGE

The first impression we make is often digital. That was true five years ago. COVID accelerated the phenomena. People will make broad, and sometimes false, assumptions about who you are and what you believe based on glimpses of your social media. It's critical that you guard, even curate, your digital image. Make sure that what you publish presents an accurate and flattering picture.

Leana Kaplan, Colorado State University

On a Sunday afternoon in the fall of 2019 a Colorado State freshman named Leana Kaplan posted a picture to her Snapchat account. It showed her and three other students wearing mud masks. Their wrists were crossed in front of their chests. Kaplan added a caption that read "Wakanda forevaa."

A picture of a few friends having a home spa day would be noncontroversial. But the totality of the image—darkened faces on White students combined with a quote and a hand gesture from a movie with a largely African American cast—obviously, drastically changed the context. The mud became Blackface. The pictured became presumed racists. And Kaplan, as the content creator, was at the center of it all.

Kaplan's snap was initially shared with a small group of her friends. Someone took a screenshot and reposted the picture with the caption "sad how you think this is okay @leana.kco." That post quickly went viral. Students began complaining to the administration. On Tuesday the president of the university made a statement denouncing the post but declaring that, because of the First Amendment, the students in the picture wouldn't be punished. This led to protests and an online petition demanding that CSU's leadership be held accountable. By Friday the story was national news.[25]

Kaplan eventually released a statement explaining what happened. She said that one of her friends got a free sample of facial mud and they were all just goofing off in the dorm trying it on. "Without it being our intention," she wrote, "we were suddenly a group in blackface. The stupidity evolved into silliness when one of the guys recited 'Wakanda forever' from the movie Black Panther, and we made the movie's crossed arms salute."

She continued "I am guilty of insensitivity and stupidity, but these do not make me a racist nor even a denier of my racism."[26] I wholeheartedly agree with part of her statement. She was incredibly stupid. Her father agreed. In an interview he said, "They're just a bunch of kids having fun and not thinking."[27] Not thinking is the problem. If

FIGURE 6.4   The photo posted by Leana Kaplan.

Kaplan had reflected for a moment before posting, she might have realized the implications of the imagery she was sharing. Instead, her recklessness cost her dearly.

She lost her part-time job.[28] She got more than 50[29] death threats. She feared enough for her safety that she moved out of her residence hall.[30] Most importantly, she gained national notoriety for doing something racist. This incident will likely follow her for the rest of her life. And it was 100% self-inflicted. Avoid Kaplan's kind of stupidity. Pause before you post anything online. Think about how someone who's never met you might react. If what you're about to publish could cast you in a bad light, refrain.

Hazel Juco, John Glenn High School, Michigan

There are times when stirring up trouble is absolutely justified. Hazel Juco's story is a good example of offending with purpose. In the fall of her senior year, she took a picture of the yellow water coming from a sink at her high school. She posted the shot on Facebook and Twitter voicing complaints about the conditions on campus. "I always hope that someone will see it and help us, because our school obviously doesn't have money," she said.

The student code of conduct prohibited cell phone use in bathrooms, locker rooms, and other private places. That's a reasonable rule. And Juco clearly violated it. The photo was obviously taken in a restroom. But there was, really, nothing wrong with what Juco did. The purpose of the cell phone ban was to protect student privacy, not insulate the administration from criticism. Still, using the phone policy as justification, Juco was handed a three-day suspension for her post. On top of that, the bathroom ban was enforced inconsistently. As Juco said, "Every girl takes selfies in the bathroom and makes it their profile pictures. No one has gotten in trouble."[31] When word of the suspension got out, parents and students in the district were outraged. They thought that school should be more focused on fixing the plumbing than punishing the student who

FIGURE 6.5   The photo Juco posted to Facebook and Twitter.

complained.[32] Dozens of Juco's friends responded to the hypocrisy by retweeting bathroom pictures they'd posted without any punishment.[33]

Juco's experience made national news. Her story was covered by CNN, *Teen Vogue*, *Seventeen* magazine, and dozens of other media outlets. Eventually the school reversed course. The superintendent admitted that Juco's punishment was inappropriate, and the suspension was expunged from her record. The plumbing was also quickly fixed.[34] When asked about all the attention, Juco said, "It's been great having all this good feedback. The bad feedback is good too, I take everything as a lesson and try to learn from everything that comes my way. And always remind myself, 'don't let it get to your head!'"[35] What a great kid. She called out the unsafe conditions at her school and didn't back down when the administration unfairly penalized her. Juco's "offensive" posts are the kind I fully support.

PROTECTING YOUR DIGITAL IMAGE

Know There Are Cameras Everywhere

Your most insensitive moment will probably be caught on camera. Keep that reality in the back of your mind even on crazy drunken nights. What you do and say could be shared, sometimes widely. And those images could reappear years from now.

Offend Intentionally

There are plenty of things wrong with the world. Pushing for change may create some pushback. You can't avoid upsetting some people; that's not possible. Instead offend purposefully and strategically.

Step Outside of Yourself

Before posting anything that might be controversial, step back and look with fresh eyes. Think about the worst way it could be misinterpreted. If there's chance you could be misread, clarify your content. When in doubt, simply don't post.

Realize Times Change

The internet has a long memory. Think long term. If a post is teetering on the tasteful/distasteful line in the present day, there's a good chance it'll be wildly inappropriate 10 years from now.

CHAPTER SUMMARY

Students have few online privacy rights. The Fourth Amendment is the law that guarantees freedom from unreasonable searches and seizures. It only applies to public schools. Private schools aren't bound by the Bill of Rights. Even at public schools, there are so many qualifiers and caveats to the Fourth Amendment, it's practically useless on a college campus. Colleges generally have a right to view anything their students post online. They can use whatever they find as evidence in an on-campus disciplinary hearing. And, since the standard of proof is so low in those hearings, a single picture can be enough to find a student guilty.

Anonymous apps and sites have been popular on college campuses for 15 years. There are upsides to these anonymous forums, but group mentality, deindividuation, and a lack of accountability push some users toward dangerous behaviors. This has happened since the dawn of the internet and continues today. And anonymous apps aren't truly anonymous. There's always some kind of digital fingerprint left behind by the posters. Any time threats have been published on anonymous sites or apps, the authorities have been able to quickly find, and arrest, the culprits.

Most employers check applicants' social media accounts before hiring. Assume anything you publish online will be seen by someone who's deciding whether to hire you, now and in the future. Alexi McCammond's story illustrates this well. She was offered a prestigious job at Condé Nast. But racist and homophobic tweets from 10 years earlier resurfaced after her appointment was announced, and she lost the job.

For certain purposes our digital personas are just as important as our real world lives. Students need to protect their online images. Before posting anything potentially controversial, step back and look with fresh eyes. If something could be misinterpreted to cast you in a bad light, recalibrate the message, or refrain.

NOTES

1   U.S. Constitution, Amendment IV.
2   Riley v. California, 573 U.S. 373 (2014).
3   Carpenter v. United States, 585 U.S. ___ (2018).
4   KATZ v. U.S., 386 U.S. 954 (1967).

5   "Electronic Privacy, Section 2.3 Investigations." *Iowa State University*, effective 8 November 2012, updated 14 June 2021.

6   "Information Technology Acceptable Use Policy, Guiding Principles." *Earlham University*, revised 26 May 2015.

7   "Information Technology Policies: Acceptable Use, Section 7. No Expectation of Privacy." *Connecticut State Colleges and Universities*, revised 31 August 2017.

8   Mapp v. Ohio, 367 U.S. 643 (1961).

9   28 U.S.C. §901.

10   Nash v. Auburn, 812 F.2d 655 (1987).

11   "Juicycampus Shuts Down, Kills the College Grapevine." *Los Angeles Times*, 4 February 2009, https://www.latimes.com/archives/blogs/technology-blog/story/2009-02-04/juicycampus-shuts-down-kills-the-college-grapevine.

12   Saveski, Martin, et al. "Tracking the Yak: An Empirical study of Yik Yak." *International AAAI Conference on Web and Social Media, North America*, 2016.

13   Diener, E., et al. "Effects of Deindividuation Variables on Stealing among Halloween Trick-or-Treaters." *Journal of Personality and Social Psychology*, vol. 33, no. 2, 1976, pp. 178–183. doi:10.1037/0022-3514.33.2.178.

14   Rhiengold, Howard. *The Virtual Community: Homesteading on the Electronic Frontier, the Edge.* Basic Books, 1993.

15   Broderick, Ryan. "Women's Rights Activist Charged with Rape Threat Hoax on Facebook." *Buzzfeed News*, 1 May 2013, https://www.buzzfeednews.com/article/ryanhatesthis/womens-rights-activist-charged-with-rape-threat-hoax-on-face.

16   Associated Press. "Ex-UW Student Accused of Fabricating Threat. *Casper Star Tribune*, 22 November 2013, https://trib.com/news/state-and-regional/ex-uw-student-accused-of-fabricating-threat/article_543e7d37-bd96-5155-93a8-e385b9c3f347.html.

17   Fleming, Megan. "Student Responsible for HUB Shooting Threat Sentenced." *Onward State*, 29 May 2015, https://onwardstate.com/2015/05/29/man-responsible-for-hub-shooting-threat-sentenced/.

18   Nersten, Colleen. "Penn State Student Charged for Allegedly Posting Bomb Threat on Yik Yak." *Onward State*, 31 August 2022, https://onwardstate.com/2022/08/31/penn-state-student-charged-for-allegedly-posting-bomb-threat-on-yik-yak/.

19   Trujillo, Trevor T. "Lanker-Simons Files Motion to Suppress Evidence in UW Crushes Case." *KOWB*, 9 July 2013, https://kowb1290.

com/lanker-simons-files-motion-to-suppress-evidence-in-uw-crushes-case/.

20 McCarthy, Erin. "Police Recount 'Intense' Search, Arrest of Student in HUB Shooting Threat." *Daily Collegian*, 13 October 2014, https://www.collegian.psu.edu/news/crime_courts/police-recount-intense-search-arrest-of-student-in-hub-shooting-threat/article_e37557ec-5351-11e4-bb98-001a4bcf6878.html.

21 Journal Record Staff. "Survey: Social Media Effective for Screening Applicants." *The Journal Record*, 14 October 2020.

22 "More than Half of Employers Have Found Content on Social Media That Caused Them Not to Hire a Candidate, According to Recent CareerBuilder Survey." Career Builder, 9 August 2018, https://press.careerbuilder.com/2018-08-09-More-Than-Half-of-Employers-Have-Found-Content-on-Social-Media-That-Caused-Them-NOT-to-Hire-a-Candidate-According-to-Recent-Career-Builder-Survey.

23 kstewart. "Nabj Names Alexi McCammond 2019 Emerging Journalist of the Year." *NABJ*, 24 June 2019, https://nabjonline.org/blog/aleximccammond2019ejoy/.

24 Robertson, Katie. "Teen Vogue Editor Resigns after Fury over Racist Tweets." *New York Times*, 18 March 2021, https://www.nytimes.com/2021/03/18/business/media/teen-vogue-editor-alexi-mccammond.html.

25 Cullor, Ravyn. "What Happened and When: A Timeline of the Blackface Incident Last Week." *Daily Collegian*, 13 September 2019, *https://collegian.com/articles/news/2019/09/what-happened-and-when-a-timeline-of-the-blackface-incident-last-week/*.

26 Kyle, Sarah. "Here's the Full Statement of the CSU Student Who Was Photographed in Viral Blackface Photo." *The Coloradan*, 13 September 2019, https://www.coloradoan.com/story/news/2019/09/13/colorado-state-university-blackface-photo-student-viral-photo-releases-full-statement/2314453001/.

27 Konopasek, Michael. "One CSU Student Seen in Blackface in Social Media Post Says She Regrets Her Decision." *Fox31 Denver*, 12 September 2019, https://kdvr.com/news/local/one-csu-student-seen-in-blackface-in-social-media-post-says-she-regrets-her-decision/.

28 Kyle, "Here's the Full Statement of the CSU Student."

29 Ferrier, Pat, and Sarah Kyle. "CSU Student in Blackface Photo: Viral Post Was 'Act of Poor Judgment during a Moment of Silliness.'" *The Coloradan*, 13 September 2019, https://www.coloradoan.

com/story/news/2019/09/13/colorado-state-university-black-face-photo-father-student-says-she-isnt-racist/2312119001/.

30   Konopasek, "One CSU Student Seen in Blackface."

31   Russell, Kim. "Student Suspended after Posting Picture of Discolored Water in School Bathroom to Social Media." *WXYZ Detroit*, 23 September 2016, https://www.wxyz.com/news/national/student-suspended-after-posting-picture-of-discolored-water-in-school-bathroom-to-social-media-1.

32   Zenteno, Rolando. "Student Suspended after She Takes Picture of School's Dirty Water." CNN, 26 September 2015, https://www.cnn.com/2016/09/26/health/school-dirty-water-post-teen-trnd/index.html.

33   Russell, "Student Suspended."

34   Ibid.

35   "Hazel Juco and John Glenn Water Update." Westland Community News, Facebook, 28 September 2016, https://www.facebook.com/WestlandNews/posts/hazel-juco-and-john-glenn-water-update-its-been-over-a-week-since-john-glenn-sen/1353805864630772/.

Credits

PART IV

DRUGS, ALCOHOL, AND PARTIES

College students regularly violate drug and alcohol laws.[1] But few have read the statutes they're breaking, let alone taken the time to really understand how they work. We'll remedy that in the following sections by examining how the laws governing underage drinking, fake IDs, and drugs operate. Beyond the legal dangers, we'll discuss how the use of drugs or alcohol can compromise your safety.

That concept—staying safe—is the touchstone of the next two chapters. Everything the law prohibits, every rule your school imposes on you, every boring, preachy lecture you've ever gotten about responsible use (including this one) has a singular goal: keeping you safe. The rules aren't designed to keep you from having fun. They exist to keep you from hurting yourselves. Keep safety in the front of your mind when reading the next section. Being on the right side of the law is important. Making sure you and your friends are healthy is infinitely more so.

---

1   "2020 National Survey on Drug Use and Health, Table 6.24, Illicit Drug Use/Misuse." U.S. Department of Health and Human Services, Substance Abuse and Mental Health Services Administration, 11 January 2022.

7 DRUG AND ALCOHOL BASICS

ALCOHOL LAWS

Underage Drinking Laws

Laws often make simple concepts as complicated as possible. This is especially true with minors and alcohol. Legally there are three components to underage drinking—possession, consumption, and internal possession (having alcohol in your system). Possession is illegal in all 50 states and the District of Columbia. The other two? It depends on where you are. Some states don't explicitly prohibit consumption. They only outlaw possession, then define it more broadly to include alcohol that's inside someone's body. Some explicitly make consumption and internal possession illegal but define those terms vaguely. Some states don't define them at all. Underage drinking statutes are a mess. They're overly complicated, hard to understand, and sometimes have conflicting sections.

Arkansas's statute illustrates this perfectly. This is the main part of the law:

> Purchase or possession by minor.
> (a) (1) It is unlawful for any person under twenty-one (21) years of age to purchase or have in his or her possession any intoxicating liquor, wine, or beer.
>
> (2) For the purposes of this section, intoxicating liquor, wine, or beer in the body of a person under twenty-one (21) years of age is deemed to be in his or her possession.[1]

Look at how this law is constructed. Part (a)(1) says it's illegal for someone under 21 to have alcohol "in his or her possession." There is no mention of consumption. Then part (a)(2) says that if someone has alcohol in their body, that counts as "possession," which effectively criminalizes consumption. Why is it written like this? I can't see any good reason. Why not simply add the word "consumption" to the first section and delete the whole second clause? There's also no mention of how internal possession is supposed to be detected or measured. Is it blood alcohol content, a urine test, something else? What levels are illegal? I'm assuming that, since the statute doesn't list a minimum allowable BAC, trace amounts would qualify. Presumably, then, a dose of NyQuil could result in a charge.

Find your state's underage drinking law. It'll look at least a little something like the Arkansas statute. Here are some of the parts you may, or may not, find in it.

Consumption, Possession, Internal Possession

Possession of alcohol is illegal in every state. Those clauses are the most straightforward. The consumption and internal possession sections are much more complicated and varied. Thirty-six states explicitly prohibit consumption in their statutes. Maryland's law is a good example:

> § 10-114. Underage possession.
>
> (a) Prohibition.- Except as provided in subsection (b)(1) of this section, and subject to subsection (b)(2) of this section, an individual under the age of 21 years may not:
> (1) possess or have under the individual's charge or control an alcoholic beverage unless the individual is a bona fide employee of the license holder as defined in Article 2B, § 1-102 of the Code and the alcoholic beverage is in the possession or under the charge or control of the individual in the course of the individual's employment and during regular working hours; or
> (2) consume an alcoholic beverage.[2]

The language in the last line is plain. But note that, like the Arkansas law, there's no explanation of how the consumption is supposed to be detected or measured. Eight states have laws like the Arkansas and Maryland statutes that prohibit internal possession but make no mention of blood alcohol content or urinalysis.

Wyoming's law is better. It says that "no person under the age of twenty-one (21) years shall ... have measurable blood, breath or urine alcohol concentration in his body."[3] Ten states have similar statutes that prohibit internal possession and actually define the term. In North Dakota the law simply says that minors can't "consume or have recently consumed"[4] alcohol. Presumably this refers to having a measurable BAC, but it's vague at best.

There are a few states that prohibit internal consumption but approach the concept in an unusual way. Washington State's underage drinking statute says that

> (b) it is unlawful for a person under the age of twenty-one years to be in a public place, or to be in a motor vehicle in a public place, while exhibiting the effects of having consumed liquor. For purposes of this subsection, exhibiting the effects of having consumed liquor means that a person has the odor of liquor on his or her breath and either: (i) Is in possession of or close proximity to a container that has or recently had liquor in it; or (ii) by speech, manner, appearance, behavior, lack of coordination, or otherwise, exhibits that he or she is under the influence of liquor.[5]

Yes, you read that correctly. A minor can't act drunk in Washington State. The law was probably drafted this way to allow the police to charge minors that they "knew" were drinking without having to breathalyze them. To me that seems like a dangerous level of latitude.

Exceptions

Religious

About half the states allow minors to possess or consume alcohol as a part of a religious ceremony. Nebraska's underage drinking laws don't apply to minors who "consume, possess, or have physical control of alcoholic liquor as a part of a bona fide religious rite, ritual, or ceremony."[6] Don't get any bright ideas about declaring your next party a "religious ceremony" and ducking the law. Your fraternity isn't a bona fide religion, even if you wear ridiculous ceremonial outfits and sometimes speak in Latin.

Parental Permission and/or Location

Several states carve out exemptions that allow minors to drink in their parents' presence or in private locations. Sometimes both need to be true for the exemption to apply. Texas allows minors to drink "in the visible presence of his adult parent, guardian, or spouse."[7] Technically that means a parent could order a beer in a bar and hand it to their child. If they maintain sight lines with their underage kid, no one would be breaking the law. In practice most bars wouldn't allow this (they have a right to refuse service).

Alaska allows minors to drink alcohol that's given "by a parent to the parent's child, by a guardian to the guardian's ward, or by a person to the legal spouse of that person if the furnishing or delivery occurs off licensed premises."[8] This means that a minor can drink anywhere that's not licensed to sell alcohol if their adult parent, guardian, or spouse gave them the liquor.

Maine's law is more restrictive, stating that minors can't drink "except in a home in the presence of the minor's parent, legal guardian or custodian."[9] The drinking must be in a home, not just off licensed premises. Minnesota has an even narrower exemption, stating that "it is an affirmative defense to a violation of this clause that the defendant consumed the alcoholic beverage in the household of the defendant's parent or guardian and with the consent of the parent or guardian."[10] Minors in the Gopher State can drink only in their family's home and with their parent's express consent.

Educational and Occupational

Almost every state specifically allows minors to possess (not consume) alcohol as a part of their jobs. This allows servers who aren't 21 yet to bring drinks to tables. In some states 18-year-olds can even work as bartenders. Several states also allow minors to possess alcohol when they're helping the police in sting operations. Oregon's underage possession laws don't apply if the minor is acting "under the direction of state or local law enforcement agencies for the purpose of investigating possible violations of laws prohibiting sales of alcoholic beverages to persons who are under 21 years of age." [11]

A few states even have exemptions for educational purposes. Florida allows "the tasting of alcoholic beverages by a student who is at least 18 years of age, who is tasting the alcoholic beverages as part of the student's required curriculum at a postsecondary educational institution."[12]

Medical

A handful of states allow minors to possess or consume alcohol if it's part of a medical treatment. Connecticut's statue specifically exempts "a minor who possesses alcoholic liquor on the order of a practicing physician."[13] I've never been prescribed a weekend of drinking by my doctor. Maybe you'll be more fortunate.

Good Samaritan Exceptions

Most states have laws on the books that grant immunity for underage drinking infractions if the offender sought help for someone in medical danger. Often, they include a few other caveats. Nevada's amnesty statute is a good example:

> 3. A person under 21 years of age is not subject to the criminal penalty set forth in subsection 1 for consuming an alcoholic beverage or subsection 2 if the person requests emergency medical assistance for another person whom he or she reasonably believes is under 21 years of age if the person making the request:
>
> (a) Reasonably believes that the person who consumed the alcohol is in need of such assistance because of the alcohol consumption;
>
> (b) Is the first person to request emergency medical assistance for the person;
>
> (c) Remains with the person until informed that his or her presence is no longer necessary by the emergency medical personnel who respond to the request for assistance for the person; and
>
> (d) Cooperates with any provider of emergency medical assistance, any other health care provider who assists the person who may be in need of emergency medical assistance because of alcohol consumption and any law enforcement officer.[14]

Under this law, in order to gain immunity, the underage drinker has to be the first person to call for help, must stay until help arrives, and must cooperate with the EMTs and law enforcement while on the scene. These are common requirements for amnesty. They're also the right thing to do when a friend is in danger.

Sometimes these amnesty clauses are included in the underage drinking section of the law. Sometimes they're stand-alone statutes and cover both drug and alcohol crimes. I think every state, and every college, should have a policy like this in place. Thankfully most do. And on campuses or in jurisdictions in which there's no written policy police officers, prosecutors, and administrators are usually willing to excuse minor crimes when an offender risked arrest in order to help another. In any case, the prospect of legal trouble should never be part of the calculus when someone's in danger. If a friend needs medical attention, get them help as fast as you can. Worry about the rest later.

Penalties

The penalties for possession, internal possession, and consumption vary as much as the governing statutes themselves. Depending on where you are, you could face fines, mandatory counseling or alcohol education, and community service, and you could lose your driver's license.

Some states are lenient. Maine has some of the lowest penalties for underage drinkers. Possessing and consuming liquor under the age of 21 is considered a civil violation and simply carries a fine $200 400 for the first offense.[15]

On the other end of the spectrum is California. A first offense for underage consumption or possession of alcohol carries a $250 fine and the offender will also have to complete at least 24 hours of community service. And, if you get caught drinking underage in the Golden State, you'll have your driver's license suspended for one year.[16]

Most states (34 at the time of writing) penalize underage drinking with license revocations. In some states it's mandatory; in others the judge has the discretion to decide whether to take the minor's license away. The lengths of suspension range from one month to a year (or multiple years for repeat offenders).

Note that, in these states, the offense itself doesn't have to involve a car to result in a loss of license. You don't have to drive a car, be in a car, near a car, or even think of car when imbibing to trigger a suspension. The simple fact that you drank before you were 21 will cost you your license. This trend started in the 1990s as an ancillary to the war on drugs. State governments have started to rethink this. They've realized that license revocations are barriers to rehabilitation and success. Given that, several states have changed their laws in the past few years and removed the license suspensions from the penalties.

Your School's Policies

Your college's rules are of paramount importance for the next few years. And the time to understand these policies is before you're accused of breaking them. Read through your school's rules about alcohol. The good news: The campus alcohol policy is probably a lot better written, and a lot easier to understand, than your state's statute. The bad news: Depending on the type of college you attend, it could say almost anything.

Campus approaches to alcohol run the gamut from incredibly restrictive (e.g., dry campuses) to very permissive. One thing to look for are location-specific rules. For example, most colleges allow students over 21 to possess and consume alcohol in their residence hall rooms. But there can be complicated caveats. Some schools require that if anyone's drinking alcohol, everyone in the room must also be of age. That means you could get in trouble just for sitting next to your 21-year-old friend while she's enjoying an adult beverage.

There are lots of variations on that theme. Rules about dry buildings or the number of students allowed in a room if alcohol's being served are common. Every campus has its policy foibles. It's your job to understand them.

Underage Purchase

Every state in the nation, except Oklahoma, has a law that specifically prohibits purchasing alcohol before you're 21. Even in Oklahoma, it's illegal to possess alcohol in "any public street, road, or highway or in any public building or place."[17] So, a minor in Oklahoma would have to magically transport the six-pack they just bought to their home without possessing it to avoid breaking the law. Still, it's strange that the purchase isn't directly addressed in their statute.

Most other states simply include purchasing alongside consumption or possession. Pennsylvania's statute says that a "person commits a summary offense if he, being less than 21 years of age, attempts to purchase, purchases, consumes, possesses or knowingly and intentionally transports any liquor."[18] Notice that Pennsylvania prohibits both the purchase and the attempted purchase of alcohol. Attempted purchase is illegal in 38 states.

A few states approach underage purchase more obtusely. They don't specifically mention purchasing, but instead make it a crime to lie about your age to obtain alcohol. Indiana's law says,

> It is a Class C misdemeanor for a minor to knowingly or intentionally make a false statement of the minor's age or to present or offer false or fraudulent evidence of majority or identity to a permittee for the purpose of ordering,

> purchasing, attempting to purchase, or otherwise pro-
> curing or attempting to procure an alcoholic beverage.[19]

Just walking up to the counter at the liquor store with a bottle of schnapps and sliding a $20 bill to the guy behind the register could qualify as making a false statement of age. Delaware, New York, and Vermont have laws like Indiana's.

Penalties for purchase and attempted purchase closely align with those for possession and consumption. You can expect fines, community service, counseling, alcohol education courses, and license suspension if you get caught.

Fake IDs

A 2021 survey conducted by Ohio State's school paper, *The Lantern*, found that almost 70% of OSU students had fake IDs.[20] That number seems high. I suspect some reporting bias. Still, it's safe to assume that a lot of college students have fakes—if for no other reason that they're exceedingly easy to buy online. Their ubiquity and accessibility might make you think that having, and using, a fake ID is no big deal, that the worst fallout of getting caught would be getting turned away from a bar. Sometimes that's all that'll happen. But you do put yourself in serious legal jeopardy when you use a fake. Actually, just possessing one can lead to serious charges in most states.

Unsurprisingly Florida, the unofficial spring break capital of the world, has a comprehensive fake ID law:

> 322.212 Unauthorized possession of, and other unlawful acts
> in relation to, driver license or identification card.—
> (1) It is unlawful for any person to:
> (a) Knowingly have in his or her possession or to
> display any blank, forged, stolen, fictitious,
> counterfeit, or unlawfully issued driver license
> or identification card or any instrument in the
> similitude of a driver license or identification
> card unless possession by such person has been
> duly authorized by the department;
>
> (b) Knowingly have in his or her possession any
> instrument in the similitude of a driver license
> issued by the department or its duly authorized
> agents or those of any state or jurisdiction issu-
> ing licenses recognized in this state for the
> operation of a motor vehicle;

> (c) Knowingly have in his or her possession any instrument in the similitude of an identification card issued by the department or its duly authorized agents or those of any state or jurisdiction issuing identification cards recognized in this state for the purpose of indicating a person's true name and age; or
>
> (d) Knowingly sell, manufacture, or deliver, or knowingly offer to sell, manufacture, or deliver, a blank, forged, stolen, fictitious, counterfeit, or unlawfully issued driver license or identification card, or an instrument in the similitude of a driver license or identification card, unless that person is authorized to do so by the department. A violation of this section may be investigated by any law enforcement agency, including the Division of Alcoholic Beverages and Tobacco.[21]

The law goes on to broadly define "driver license" and "identification card" to include any document from any state that shows someone's name and age.

Florida classifies most false ID infractions as felonies in the third degree. For reference, other third-degree felonies in Florida include stealing a car or trespassing while armed. The maximum penalty is five years in prison and a fine of $5,000.[22] This is much worse than a doorman at the local dive hassling you.

Not every state is as harsh as Florida. In Arizona simple possession of a fake ID is a class 2 misdemeanor,[23] punishable by up to four months in prison[24] and a $750 fine.[25] If you use the fake ID to purchase liquor or get into a bar it becomes a class 1 misdemeanor.[26] Those can result in a $2,500 fine[27] and six months in jail.[28] There's also a mandatory license suspension of six months for using a fake ID in Arizona.

Generally, the penalties for using a fake ID are worse than for simple possession. And there are ancillary crimes that could be pursued by local law enforcement if they chose to. Technically, if someone under the age of 21 fraudulently gains access to a bar, they're trespassing. And, depending on the circumstances, identity theft statutes could apply. There's even a possibility of forgery charges if you made your own ID or altered a state license.

Just lending your license to a friend could lead to serious trouble. In Illinois, for example, it's a class A misdemeanor to "knowingly duplicate, manufacture, sell or transfer any fraudulent identification card."[29] Handing your ID to a buddy is "transferring" a fraudulent ID. Class A misdemeanors carry a fine of up to $2,500 and up to a year in jail in Illinois.[30]

As with all laws, the penalties, the structures of the statutes, and enforcement levels vary by state and sometimes locality. No matter where you live, using a fake ID is probably a more serious crime than you think it is.

Selling Fakes

Selling or manufacturing fake IDs moves you into the criminal major leagues. Still, enterprising but foolish college students keep getting caught selling forged documents to their friends. One of the largest recent criminal rings operated out of the University of Georgia in 2010 and 2011.

In the fall of 2009 William Trosclair, a freshman at UGA, met Tyler Ruby, a Gainesville State student. Ruby was already making and selling fake IDs on a small scale before the two met. Trosclair wanted one for himself but didn't have the money. Ruby offered him a deal. If Trosclair brought in 10 sales from his friends, Ruby would make him an ID for free.

Trosclair easily found 10 clients at UGA, got his own fake for free, and because he charged a premium, made a quick $200. That was the start of Ruby and Trosclair's partnership. Over the next few semesters, the business grew quickly, as did the quality of the fakes they sold. They bought a $3,000 card printer and even managed to buy some official state holograms from an overseas vendor.

Friends and former clients kept referring new business to the pair. They eventually had students selling for them at 10 other schools, including Northwestern, the University of Alabama, and Ole Miss. Trosclair, flush with cash from his forgery ring, lived the high life. He picked up huge tabs at bars and organized outings to strip clubs where he'd hand out one-dollar bills to his buddies. He was like a dumber, poorer wolf of Wall Street.

Things began to unravel in August of 2011 when another UGA student reported her roommate, who was one of Trosclair and Ruby's salespeople, to her RA. That triggered an investigation that ended with Ruby and Trosclair each being charged with 16 felony counts of manufacturing a false identification. Nineteen other students who sold or delivered the IDs were indicted on lesser counts. During the investigation police confiscated roughly 600 fake IDs manufactured by the pair. They estimate the actual number sold was closer to 2,000.[31]

The foot soldiers of the operation were all accepted into a first-time offender program. They had to pay a $1,000 fine and complete 100 hours of community service. Ruby and Trosclair both reached plea deals. They were sentenced to two to four months in prison, a $5,000 fine, and 100 hours of community service.[32] Trosclair initially tried to fight the charges—his father even sold his construction business to pay the legal fees. But in the end, he decided that pleading out was his best option. [33]

A $5,000 fine and a few months behind bars is a serious sentence. In my opinion, though, Ruby and Trosclair were lucky. Had they been charged under the federal law they would have been facing a 15-year sentence.[34] Given the magnitude of their enterprise they could, and maybe should, have been imprisoned for much longer.

A final note: Most of us only think of fake IDs in relation to buying alcohol. The truth of the matter is much darker. Fraudulent documents are associated with public benefit fraud, identity theft, human trafficking, and terrorism.[35] At the very least, before you click "buy" and order a fake from some offshore provider, think for a moment about the industry you're supporting. I understand that you want to party with your friends. But when you purchase a fraudulent ID there's a very real chance that you're sending money to an organization that aids in the kidnapping and sale of human beings or that helps terrorists and other criminals evade travel security screenings.

DRUG LAWS

Marijuana Laws

Underage drinking laws are confusing mostly due to poor draftsmanship. In contrast, marijuana laws are muddled by vastly different enforcement schemes in neighboring—and overlapping—jurisdictions. The biggest problem is the fact that the federal government still considers all marijuana illegal. It's listed as a Schedule I drug, putting it on par with cocaine and heroin. But 37 states have legalized the use of marijuana for medical purposes, and 20 now allow recreational use. People who use (or grow or sell) weed legally under state laws are technically simultaneously violating federal law.

This has wide-reaching implications. According to the U.S. Constitution, if state and federal law are in conflict, federal law wins (the

Supremacy Clause). But police powers are delegated to states via the 10th Amendment. This means that states can largely control enforcement, but they probably couldn't stop the federal government from prosecuting marijuana crimes in the federal courts if push came to shove. The current state of things is precarious at best.

For you, as college students, this state and federal distinction is incredibly important. Schools, both public and private, must follow federal laws. This means that colleges can't allow marijuana on their property. No matter where you live, no matter what kind of college you go to, you're not allowed to possess or use marijuana on campus. It's just that simple. Hopefully this conflict will be cleared up soon and the federal restrictions will be lifted. Aside from preventing students in weed-friendly states from enjoying it on campus, the current scheme has stunted research into marijuana.

This conflict also makes crossing state lines with marijuana dangerous. Of course, you can't buy weed in a jurisdiction in which it's legal then bring it to a state where possession is still criminal. Technically, even transporting marijuana across any state line, even between two states where it's been decriminalized, violates federal law. Because once something travels between two states it enters in what's called interstate commerce, and federal statutes apply.

Prescription Drugs

Nearly a third (28.1%) of college-aged adults say they have misused prescription psychotherapeutic drugs at least once in their lifetime. That's an astonishingly high number. It's also part of an alarming upward trend. In 1996 only 9.6% reported that kind of abuse. It rose to 14.6% in 2006.[36] It's a safe bet that with the added stress of the COVID era misuse will continue to rise in the short-term future.

Adderall, Ritalin, Concerta, and other ADHD drugs have a reputation among college students as being "smart drugs" that help you study. Students think they'll have better focus and that their grades will go up if they take these pills. That's untrue. Studies show that although Adderall "may aid in the enhancements of some aspects of learning, it is not a reliable study aid."[37]

In other words, the pills you're getting from your roommate or buying from some "source" (which is incredibly dangerous—we'll get to that in a moment) probably aren't having the intended effect. What's worse, using these drugs without a prescription puts you in serious legal jeopardy.

Legal Implications

In the spring of 2013, during midterms, two students met up in the lobby of the student center at the University of Colorado at Boulder. One of the students took a tablet of Vyvanse (a stimulant) out of a bottle and handed it the other, who gave him $5 in return. It's a scene that probably plays out tens of thousands of times on campuses every day. These two students happened to catch the eye of a nearby university employee. That employee approached the two students, detained them, and contacted campus police.

The selling student was charged with the unlawful sale of a controlled substance, a felony. If convicted, he could have faced a maximum sentence of a year in prison and up to $100,000 in fines. The buyer was also charged with a felony, unlawful possession of a controlled substance, which carries the same sentence. Both pled down to the petty offense of possession of drug paraphernalia and had to perform 16 hours of community service.[38]

I'm sure that neither of those students had an inkling that they were committing such a serious crime when they passed that single tablet between them. Why would they meet out in the open in the lobby of one of the busiest buildings on campus if they did? I'd bet that the thousands of students who complete similar transactions at schools across the country are also blissfully, or willfully, ignorant of the gravity of their actions.

NONLEGAL CONSEQUENCES

Violating drug laws can have far-reaching consequences beyond actual criminal penalties. Of course, you could also be subject to school discipline. Your car insurance premium could skyrocket (even for nonvehicle offenses). You could also lose some forms of federal aid—you may actually have to pay your grants back. After graduation, a conviction could prevent you from getting certain professional licenses (law, medicine, teaching, law enforcement). And having a record will hurt your job prospects in any field.

Operation Spiderweb

The law is the least of your worries when you illegally buy pharmaceuticals. The real risk is that you'll take a pill that could kill you. There's a huge demand for second-market prescription drugs. There simply isn't a big enough supply to fill the void. To meet demand, dealers manufacture fake pills—very convincing fake pills—and pass them off them as the genuine article. They're made of whatever the dealers can get their hands on. Often that means methamphetamine or fentanyl, both of which can be deadly.

Students think that if they're buying pills from someone they know, such as a classmate, they're buying authentic medicine. That's a dangerous assumption. A drug trafficking ring at the University of Texas at San Antonio illustrates this well. In 2019 San Antonio police noticed a sharp increase in drug overdoses, both on campus and in the nearby community. The culprit was an influx of thousands of fake Adderall and Xanax tablets that were laced with fentanyl and methamphetamine. Their investigation, named Operation Spiderweb, lasted more than a year and ultimately led to the arrests of 15 individuals for distribution and money laundering. There were two other suspects under surveillance who died of drug overdoses before they could be arrested.[39]

The police uncovered a vast criminal organization. Huge quantities of fentanyl, marijuana, counterfeit pills, and LSD were confiscated, along with manufacturing equipment, guns, bullet-proof vests, and $100,000 in cash. Authorities estimate that the group distributed more than $1 million worth of drugs at colleges throughout the region. Some of the pills sold were actual diverted narcotics, but most were counterfeit.

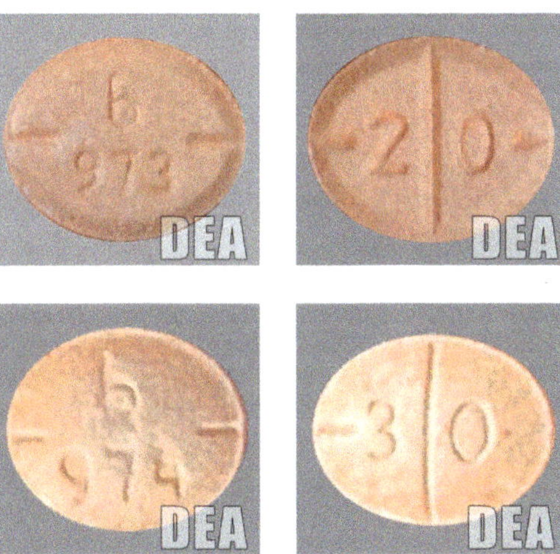

FIGURE 7.1   Authentic Adderall pills (top) and counterfeit pills (bottom).

Of the 15 arrested, 8 were former or current University of Texas at San Antonio students. The ringleader was 23-year-old Varun Prasad, who graduated from UTSA in 2019 with a bachelor's degree in mathematics.[40] The woman who was physically manufacturing many of the counterfeit pills, Rose Rodriguez-Rabin, was a professor. She had been a member of the English department for 15 years. When her apartment was raided the authorities found roughly 40,000 fake Adderall tablets (made of methamphetamine) and the equipment used to make them.[41]

There are two major takeaways from Operation Spiderweb. First, think about who these drug dealers were—students and a professor. As Steven Whipple, a DEA special agent, said when the arrests were announced, "These kids are all well-educated. We saw mathematics majors, chemistry majors, a psychology major, business majors. They decided to turn their talents into this illicit operation."[42] These were respected members of the university community who peddled fake pills to their friends on campus.

Second, think about what they were selling. The pills looked like genuine pharmaceuticals. But they were counterfeits made of meth and fentanyl. The drugs this group sold were so dangerous that two of the dealers died during course of the investigation. Again, you might think that buying pills from someone you know, such as a classmate, means what they're giving you is legitimate. But that's not the case. If it came from anywhere other than a pharmacy, it could be fake.

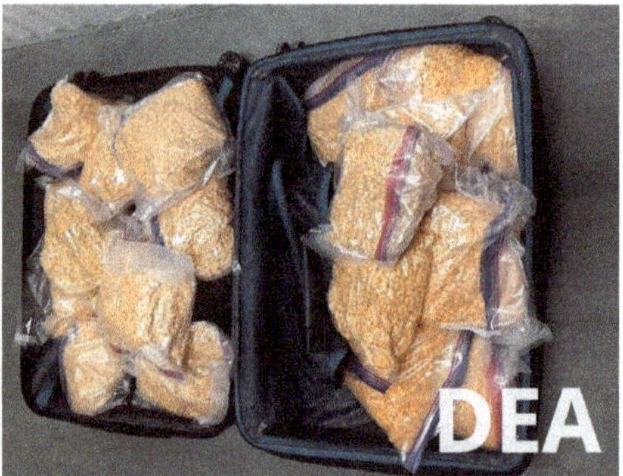

FIGURE 7.2   Equipment used to manufacture counterfeit pills and fake Adderall tablets found in the home of UTSA professor Rose Rodriguez-Rabin during Operation Spiderweb.

Over the last few years operations like the one at UTSA have been on the rise. Drug trafficking organizations have also flooded the U.S. with fake pharmaceuticals. In 2022 the DEA confiscated more than 10,000 pounds of fentanyl powder and 50.6 million illegal fentanyl tablets. That translates to more than 379 million fatal doses, enough fentanyl to kill every person in the United States.[43] Please, be incredibly careful. Only take prescription drugs that come directly from a legitimate source. The risks associated with taking bootleg pharma products are just too high.

CHAPTER SUMMARY

Legally, there are three components to underage drinking: possession, consumption, and internal possession. Possession is illegal in every state. The statutes governing consumption and internal possession vary widely by jurisdiction. Depending on where you live, one or both may be illegal. Many states also carve out exemptions. In some jurisdictions minors can drink with their parent's permission, as a part of religious ceremony, or for educational or medical purposes. Most states also offer good Samaritan exemptions. Because every state's law is unique, it's important to read and understand the local statutes. It's also critical to read your specific school's alcohol policy.

State laws governing fake IDs also vary widely. Even in the most lenient jurisdictions the penalties are more severe than one might think. Simple possession could result in jail time and large fines. Even lending a valid ID to a friend could lead to criminal charges. Selling and manufacturing false identification cards are much more serious crimes. The federal penalty for the manufacture of fake IDs is 15 years in prison.

There is currently a conflict between state and federal marijuana laws. Many states have decriminalized the use of marijuana for recreational or medicinal purposes. But the federal government still considers all marijuana illegal. Because colleges, public and private, have to follow federal law, marijuana is banned on every campus in the nation.

Although Adderall, Ritalin, and other pharmaceuticals have a reputation as "smart drugs," studies show that they're not reliable as study aids. Further, illegally possessing or selling a controlled substance is a serious crime. More importantly, the U.S. has been flooded with fake pharmaceuticals over the last few years. Many of them contain fatal doses of methamphetamine or fentanyl. In 2022 alone the DEA seized enough fentanyl to kill every person in the country. Taking any drug that hasn't come directly from a pharmacy is incredibly dangerous.

NOTES

1   AR Code § 3-3-203 (2020).
2   MD Crim. Law Code § 10-114 (2013).
3   WY Stat § 12-6-101 (2021).
4   N.D.C.C. § 5-01-018 (2020).
5   WA Rev Code § 66.44.270 (2021).
6   NE Code § 53-180.02 (2021).
7   TX Alco. Bev Code § 106.04 (2021).
8   AK Stat § 04.16.051 (2021).
9   28-A ME Rev Stat § 2051 (2021).
10   MN Stat § 340A.503 (2021).
11   OR Rev Stat § 471.430 (2021).
12   FL Stat § 562.111 (2021).
13   CT Gen Stat § 30-89 (2020).
14   NE Code § 53-180.05 (2021).
15   28-A ME Rev Stat § 2051 (2021).
16   CA Bus & Prof Code § 25662 (2021).
17   10A OK Stat § 10A-2-8-222 (2021).
18   18 PA Cons Stat § 6308 (2021).
19   IN Code § 7.1-5-7-1 (2021).
20   Czajkowski, Bella. "Fake IDs Find Popularity Regardless of Legal and University Consequences." *Ohio State Lantern*, 29 April 2021, https://www.thelantern.com/projects/2021/04/28/fake-ids-join-textbooks-and-shower-caddies-on-the-college-packing-list-find-popularity-regardless-of-legal-and-university-consequences/.
21   FL Stat § 322.212 (2021).
22   FL Stat § 775.082 (2021).
23   AZ Rev Stat § 28-3478 (2021).
24   AZ Rev Stat § 13-707 (2021).
25   AZ Rev Stat § 13-802 (2021).
26   AZ Rev Stat § 4-241 (2021).
27   AZ Rev Stat § 13-802 (2021).
28   AZ Rev Stat § 13-707 (2021).

29   15 ILCS § 335/1. Illinois Identification Card Act. (2021).

30   15 ILCS § 335/14B(b)(7)-(9) (2021).

31   Schick, David. "ID Kingpin." *The Flagpole*, 19 February 2014, https://flagpole.com/news/news-features/2014/02/19/id-kingpin/.

32   Johnson, Joe. "Confinement, Probation for Ringleaders of UGA-Based Fake ID Ring." *Athens Banner-Herald*, 21 October 2013, https://www.onlineathens.com/story/news/state/2013/10/21/confinement-probation-ringleaders-uga-based-fake-id-ring/15453081007/.

33   Schick, "ID Kingpin."

34   18 USC § 1028 (2011).

35   WLTW Digital Staff. "Cincinnati Custom Agents Seize 14,504 Fake IDs in 2020." *WLTW5*, 5 January 2021.

36   Iqbal, Mohammad M., et al. "Adderall Abuse among College Students." *Journal of Anxiety and Depression*, vol. 3, no. 1, 2020, p. 121.

37   Ibid.

38   Byars, Mitchell. "Felony Dropped as CU-Boulder Student Charged with Buying a $5 Pill Takes Plea Deal." *Daily Camera*, 19 June 2013, https://www.dailycamera.com/2013/04/11/felony-dropped-as-cu-boulder-student-charged-with-sale-of-5-pill-takes-plea-deal/.

39   Patton, Mary Claire. "Feds: Ex-UTSA Lecturer Tied to Drug Trafficking Ring That Sold Counterfeit Pills to Students in San Antonio, Austin." *KSAT*, 4 December 2020, https://www.ksat.com/news/local/2020/12/04/feds-utsa-lecturer-tied-to-drug-trafficking-ring-that-sold-counterfeit-pills-to-students-in-san-antonio-austin/.

40   Ibid.

41   Martinez, Sarah. "UTSA Lecturer Suspended after DEA Raid at Her Apartment Uncovers 40,000 Counterfeit Adderall Pills Made with Meth." *San Antonio Current*, 12 December 2020, https://www.sacurrent.com/news/utsa-lecturer-suspended-after-dea-raid-at-her-apartment-uncovers-40000-counterfeit-adderall-pills-made-with-meth-22552133.

42   Osbourne, Heather. "Feds Charge 13 in Drug Trafficking Ring That Sold to UT Students in Austin." *Austin American-Statesman*, 4 December 2021, https://www.statesman.com/story/news/crime/2020/12/04/13-charged-drug-trafficking-ring-targeting-ut-students-austin/3825291001/.

43   Miroff, Nick. "DEA Seized Enough Fentanyl to Kill Every Person in the U.S. in 2022." *Washington Post*, 20 December 2022, https://www.washingtonpost.com/national-security/2022/12/20/fentanyl-seizures-2022-dea/.

Credits

Fig. 7.1a: Source: https://www.dea.gov/onepill.
Fig. 7.1b: Source: https://www.dea.gov/onepill.
Fig. 7.1c: Source: https://www.dea.gov/onepill.
Fig. 7.1d: Source: https://www.dea.gov/onepill.
Fig. 7.2a: Source: https://www.newsnationnow.com/us-news/southwest/operation-spider-web-13-arrested-in-drug-trafficking-ring-that-sold-to-texas-college-students/?ipid=promo-link-block1.
Fig. 7.2b: Source: https://www.newsnationnow.com/us-news/southwest/operation-spider-web-13-arrested-in-drug-trafficking-ring-that-sold-to-texas-college-students/?ipid=promo-link-block1.

HOW TO THINK ABOUT YOUR PARTY

Protect Everyone's Safety

The wording of this chapter's title is your first and most important tip—safety comes before legal concerns. I want you to stay out of trouble. But making sure that no one gets hurt—or dies—is far more important. In fact, safety is the only thing that matters at all. Adopt this simple rule as your party-throwing prime directive: Once someone steps into your space, they're your responsibility. It's your job to make sure that no harm comes to them. Even after they leave, they're still in your charge. You need to guarantee that they get home, and through the night, safely.

Protect Yourself Legally

The next order of business is protecting yourself legally. That's what a lot of this chapter discusses. Be mindful of the rules and laws. That's the easy part. What's more difficult is making sure you don't get into trouble for other people's stupid actions. There are steps you can take, especially at off-campus parties, that can help legally insulate you from your guests' idiocy.

Now onto the party thrower's prep course.

BEFORE THE PARTY

Make Nice with Your Neighbors

What's the number-one reason the authorities show up at an off-campus party? Noise. The booming base or loud drunks spilling onto the street annoy a neighbor, who calls the cops. When the police show up to tell you to quiet down, they find all sorts of other laws being broken. And you find yourself in a world of legal trouble.

How do you prevent this? The first thing is get to know your neighbors. It's essential to befriend those within shouting distance. Also, do some advance public relations work by being a model neighbor. Help them bring their trash cans in. Shovel their walks when it snows. And keep the front of your house as neat as you can manage. Do what it takes to make them like you, or at the very least, not actively dislike you.

More importantly, before the party let your neighbors know you're having people over. Then ask them to call you—not the police—if things get too loud. For those of you who are bad at conversations, here's a sample script:

> Hi, my name is [insert name], and I live over at [insert address]. I'm the guy who shoveled your driveway last month. I just wanted to let you know that we're having a party on Saturday. Come by and join us if you want. But more importantly, if things get too loud or you have any other kind of problem, please give us a call. I've written down our names and phone numbers on this card as well as the time and date of the party. Thanks.

If they do call, quiet things down quickly. You're only going to get one chance to appease them. If the music stays loud after they complain, their next call will be to the police.

If you want to win extra points, never underestimate the power of a gift. Bring some cookies, a gift certificate to the local movie theater, even a crappy bottle of wine. Think of it. It's the night of the party. It's late. You and your friends are being loud. Your neighbors are annoyed and about to call the police. But then they think, "Oh no, I can't do that to that nice boy; he brought me a box of Franzia. I'll just call and ask him to quiet things down instead."

Perform a Perimeter Sound Check

Noise ordinances are local. Your town will have its own law about how loud things can get before they become illegal. Some are very specific. In College Station Texas (home of Texas A&M) the noise ordinance delineates unreasonable noise using distances and decibels:

    a. During the hours of 10:01 p.m. to 6:59 a.m. that, when measured from the property line of a residence located in residential zoned property, exceeds 56 decibels and would disturb or annoy a person of ordinary sensibilities; or

b. During the hours of 10:01 p.m. to 6:59 a.m. that, when measured from a contiguous interior wall of a residence that is a multiunit residence located in residential zoned property, exceeds 50 decibels and would disturb or annoy a person of ordinary sensibilities.[1]

Most are, purposely, written vaguely. Beloit Wisconsin's (Beloit College) law simply says, "No person shall, at any time, make any noise tending to unreasonably disturb the peace and quiet of any person in the vicinity thereof." Then it gives a few examples of what might qualify as unreasonable, including "any musical instrument, radio, television, phonograph, stereo, cassette player, compact disc player or any sound amplification equipment" that can be heard inside another house or across the street.[2] You crazy kids with your loud phonographs.

Do a sound check before your party. Turn up the stereo in the room you're planning on using. Then go outside. If you can hear it from your property line, it's too loud. This will give you an idea of how much of a racket you can make without attracting the attention of your neighbors. Use that benchmark to keep an eye on noise levels throughout the night. Noise is also the first reason (and there will be several) you should never host outdoor parties.

Invitations

When I was a student, we printed out fliers to let people know we were having people over. We'd hand them out to our friends, stuff them in mailboxes, or even post them on bulletin boards around campus. It was a bad idea on many fronts. Your generation doesn't need to rely on hard copies now that texting and social media exist. But you can still run into problems when inviting people digitally.

You need to avoid opening your party to the public at large. The concept is a bit complicated, but the law treats invitees and trespassers differently. If you make your party widely known and invite everyone on earth, you owe some legal duties to all those who show up—whether you know them or not. And they could potentially sue you if they get hurt while at your place. In some instances, you could even be held legally liable for their actions (or crimes). Invite as many people as you want, but contact them directly, not via a public Snapchat post. Also, ask your friends not to forward your invitation on to other people.

DURING THE PARTY

Party Financing

Every single state in the nation requires a liquor license to sell alcohol.

I guarantee you will be lied to about this during your time in college. Someone will tell you there's an easy way around these laws. They'll say that all you need to do is charge guests $10 for red solo cups. Then you can use that cash to pay for the keg. Or that you can impose an entrance fee to defray the cost of buying booze for all your friends. They'll smugly tell you that these and other ridiculous schemes are ironclad ways to skirt the law.

Any switch-up scheme, in which partygoers pay for something benign then the proceeds go toward alcohol, is illegal. It won't hold up in court. No magistrate in the country is going to believe that "cups cost $10 but the vodka was free."

To be extraordinarily clear you cannot do the following:

→   Charge for a cup and give away alcohol for free
→   Charge to get in and give away alcohol for free
→   Charge for a band or other entertainment and give away alcohol for free
→   Enforce mandatory "donations"

Unlawful sale statutes carry substantial penalties. In Pennsylvania fines are based on the amount of alcohol found on the premises—$2 per fluid ounce of beer and $4 per fluid ounce of wine or liquor. That's a $1,280 fine for a keg and $120 for a handle of vodka.[3] In Tennessee, selling liquor without a license is a class B misdemeanor, which carries a fine of $500 and up to six months in prison.[4]

Also, if you're caught selling liquor without a license your insurance company (or your parents' insurance company) could deny coverage. If someone gets into a car accident after drinking out of their $10 cup all night, they'll probably sue you. If your insurer can prove you were selling liquor without a license, then your family might be on their own. They might have to pay tens of thousands of dollars in legal fees, or even millions in damages, out of pocket.

Furnishing Alcohol to Minors

A citation for providing alcohol to an underaged person is one of the bigger criminal liabilities a host could face (that's different than a civil liability, see the next section). It's illegal in every state to give, sell, trade for, transfer, or provide alcohol in any way to a minor. And you don't have to be over 21 yourself to violate these laws. Generally, if you can be tried as an adult giving alcohol to another minor is a violation.

The statutes are straightforward. New Mexico's law makes it illegal to

> (1) sell, serve or give alcoholic beverages to a minor or permit a minor to consume alcoholic beverages on the licensed premises;
>
> (2) buy alcoholic beverages for or procure the sale or service of alcoholic beverages to a minor;
>
> (3) deliver alcoholic beverages to a minor; or
>
> (4) aid or assist a minor to buy, procure or be served with alcoholic beverages.[5]

The crime is a fourth-degree felony in New Mexico. It carries a maximum sentence of 18 months in prison and a $5,000 fine.[6] That may seem steep in and of itself. Now consider this: You could be charged separately for every minor you served. If there were 17 underage drinkers at your party in New Mexico, you could be looking at maximum fine of $85,000 and more than 25 years in prison—sobering, both literally and figuratively.

As with all underage drinking laws, the statutes and penalties vary widely by state. New Mexico is on the harsher end of the spectrum. Southeastern states tend to be more lenient. In South Carolina providing alcohol to someone under 21 is a misdemeanor and carries a maximum sentence of 30 days in prison and a $300 fine.[7]

POST SIGNS

Put signs up everywhere there's alcohol that say, "You must be 21 to drink alcohol at this party." Take pictures to memorialize them. They might be useful in court later as evidence that any underage drinkers were indulging against your wishes.

No matter the state, the chance of getting the maximum penalty for a first offense (or group of offenses) is functionally zero. Still, you'll likely end up with a fine and possibly probation. And, since the stakes are high, you'll need to hire (and pay) a lawyer to represent you.

Searches and Residence Hall Rooms

Residence hall rooms are bad places to throw parties.

This is the Fourth Amendment to the United States Constitution:

> The right of the people to be secure in their persons,
> houses, papers, and effects, against unreasonable searches
> and seizures, shall not be violated, and no Warrants shall
> issue, but upon probable cause, supported by Oath or
> affirmation, and particularly describing the place to be
> searched, and the persons or things to be seized.[8]

It's the law that keeps the police from coming into your apartment and searching your possessions without justification. In most cases they either need to have a warrant or your permission to search your home. The bad news for students who live in residence halls? The Fourth Amendment only applies to the police, not to resident assistants or other university employees—even at a public school.

This means an RA can come into your room without a warrant or your permission and look around. What's more, if they find evidence of a crime, they could hand it over to the police to use against you in court. The RA can't work on behalf of the cops. But if a university employee is acting on their own, any contraband found in your room is fair game in a trial.

Not every university behaves this way. Many colleges include language in their student handbooks about residence hall privacy. And a fair number hold themselves to higher standards than the law dictates. For example, the University of Nebraska's Community Living Guide says,

> The right to privacy, guaranteed by federal and state laws,
> applies to your residence hall room. Entry to student
> rooms is limited to emergency or repair circumstances as
> deemed necessary by complex staff, or as may be legally
> required.[9]

There's a lot of wiggle room in the self-imposed rules. But they're better than nothing. They give students at Nebraska Lincoln some semblance of some privacy rights in university housing units. That may not be the case at your school.

This is yet another reason you need to read and understand your school's rules and policies. Your college may have granted you some privacy rights, like UNL. Or their rules may say something along the lines of "the university reserves the right to enter any residence hall room at any time for any reason." You won't know unless you've gone through the fine print. Take the time to look at your housing contract, the residential life policy, and whatever other rules will be governing your time living on campus.

The Fourth Amendment and Off-Campus Parties

Just before midnight on September 30, 1999, a resident of Cleveland Heights, Ohio, called 911 to report a loud party up the street. The local police force sent four officers. Commander Bradford Sudyk said that when he arrived, he looked through the front window and saw three "youthful-looking" people sitting at a table drinking beer.[10]

Sudyk knocked. The three beer-drinkers saw him, jumped up, and ran to the back of the house. Eventually a different guest opened the door. Sudyk asked to talk to the owners of the home, but no one would identify the hosts. Instead, most of the partygoers ran out of the room toward the back of the building. From the threshold Sudyk could see multiple guests who were dangerously intoxicated, including someone who could hardly stand.[11]

He went into the house at that point (without a warrant or permission) and continued to ask for whoever was in charge. Eventually two men—George Namay and Lawrence Fiely—admitted that it was their place. Sudyk testified that there were roughly 75 people in the house and that most looked 18 or 19. When Sudyk asked "Who's under 21?" most of the partygoers raised their hands. After that Sudyk checked IDs and performed field sobriety tests on the entire crowd. A few of the guests were charged with underage drinking and the hosts—Namay and Fiely—were charged with disorderly conduct and serving alcohol to individuals under 21.[12]

Namay and Fiely challenged their arrests in court, arguing that because Sudyk didn't have a warrant, and no one gave the police permission to enter, the search violated the Fourth Amendment. The court upheld their arrests stating the following:

> The government presented a need for immediate action for a number of reasons: the preservation of evidence, the abatement of an ongoing nuisance, and the prevention of flight. The disturbance call established that the activity in the home was disturbing to the neighborhood. However, upon arrival of the police, the defendants refused to offer any assistance to the officers to quell the disturbance. In fact, they would neither identify themselves nor come

> to the door. It was late at night and the courts were not
> open; a warrant could not be secured quickly. ...
>
> It would be practically impossible for four officers to
> contain some 75 people within a home while a warrant
> request could be prepared and a neutral magistrate could
> be found to rule on that request well after court hours.[13]

Read through this excerpt a few times and think about what this ruling really means. My takeaway: In a college town, when the police show up at house where there's a loud party going on, they probably have a right to come in. First, they have a duty to keep the peace. If the hosts refuse to talk to the cops and quiet things down—like Namay and Fiely did—the entry would certainly be justified.

More importantly, the police must be able to enforce the law. And requiring to the cops to get a warrant before they check to see who's been drinking and who's of age, which could take hours late at night when the courts are closed, would make that impossible. Underage drinkers could flee. Even if they stayed, the alcohol in their blood may be gone by the time the warrant was obtained.

The bottom line is if you throw an off-campus party and the police show up at the front door, chances are the Fourth Amendment isn't going to protect you.

Social Host Liability

If someone leaves your party and harms themselves or someone else, you could be held legally responsible. This is called social host liability. To illustrate how this works we'll look at a 2020 New Jersey case, *Narleski v. Gomes.*

On the afternoon of November 14, 2014, Brandon Narleski bought three 24 ounces cans of beer and a 1.75-liter bottle vodka at a convenience store. He was with Mark Zwierzynski and two other friends. All four were under 21. But Brandon had a beard and looked the oldest, so he bought the alcohol. They took the beer and vodka to Zwierzynski's house (his parents weren't home) drank, watched TV, and played video games for a few hours.

Around 9:00 that night another friend, Nicholas Gomes, arrived. He quickly downed two large vodka drinks. Roughly an hour later Gomes and Narleski decided to go to a different friend's house. By this time Gomes said that he was "buzzed" and was slurring his words. Still, he drove. En route, he tried to pass another car and lost control. His

Mercedes crossed over multiple lanes of traffic and slammed into the concrete divider on the highway. Brandon was ejected from the car, which flipped over and landed on top of him. He was pronounced dead at the scene. Gomes survived. His BAC at the time of the accident was 0.16%.[14] Gomes pled guilty to vehicular homicide and was sentenced to seven years in jail.[15]

Brandon Narleski's parents sued multiple parties for the death of their son—Gomes, the store that sold him the vodka, Zwierzynski's parents. The case took a complicated legal path with multiple cross suits. But the question that eventually came to the New Jersey Supreme Court was this: Did Mark Zwierzynski have any responsibility for Brandon Narleski's death? Remember Zwierzynski was a minor himself. He didn't even buy the alcohol. Brandon did. His only actual contribution was providing a parentless house.

The Court held that yes, Zwierzynski could be held liable for Brandon's death. Zwierzynski knew that Gomes was drunk. He knew Gomes was going to drive. As the host it was his responsibility to ensure everyone's safety. Letting Gomes get behind the wheel was negligence.[16]

The Narleski case represents the latest expansion of social host liability law in New Jersey. That's the national trend—expansion, not contraction. Over the last few decades, courts and legislators have steadily moved toward more liability for social hosts. At the time of writing more than 30 states allow lawsuits against social hosts who serve minors. Even in states in which social host liability isn't officially recognized, an enterprising judge could still rule against you in some creative way. Legally, once someone has a drink at your house, or in your room, there's a good chance you'll be held liable if they hurt themself or someone else after they leave.

This is yet another area where the law is secondary. Forget about civil suits and statutes. If someone dies after leaving your party, the potential penalties will be the least of your worries. I've spoken with students—far too many—who've lost a friend after a night of drinking. Their minds are never on the law. They say they'd do anything to be able to go back in time and make different choices. They just wish their friends were still alive.

I said this at the beginning of the chapter, but it bears stating again: Once someone steps into your place and takes even a single sip of alcohol they become your responsibility. It doesn't matter where they got the booze. It doesn't matter how old you are, or they are for that matter. If they drink at your place and then get hurt, it's on you. There's a good chance the law will see it that way. And if something unthinkable does happen, I guarantee your conscience will.

Have Designated Hosts

How do you avoid this kind of trouble? Have at least two sober people at every party you throw to keep an eye out for danger—both legal and actual. If the police do arrive, you'll need someone with a clear head to talk to them. And remember, you gave your number to the neighbors. If a drunk picks up when they call, they'll probably just hang up and call the police. More importantly, bad things happen at parties. Someone with their wits about them needs to head off potential disasters and deal with the problems that do arise. The hosts' specific duties should include the following.

Watch the Entrances

You should never block exits (in case of fires), but someone should have an eye on every door all evening. You want to know who's coming into your house. And you want to ensure that drunks don't stumble off by themselves. Also, keep a trashcan near each exit and insist that everyone throws their drinks and empties out before they leave. If someone heads out onto public property with just the residue of beer or liquor in their solo cup, they could get cited for violating open container laws. This is reason number two you should never host parties outside. You also don't want a trail of drinkers, or litter, leading back your place.

Don't Let Anyone Drink and Drive

This should go without saying, but if anyone's been drinking at all, don't let them drive. Don't engage in a debate about letting them go. Be conclusive. Say, "I'm getting you an Uber," not "Are you okay to drive?" Before the party make sure you've got a ride share app on your phone and keep the number of your local taxi company (if your town has one) handy.

House Sweeps

At least once an hour—every half hour is better—go through every nook and cranny of your place to check for trouble. Inspect basements, rooms with closed doors, and the outside areas adjacent to your place. You want to make sure that everyone's accounted for and no one's in a compromising situation.

Watch for Anyone Overindulging

If anyone is exhibiting the signs of alcohol poisoning or a drug overdose, act quickly. At the first sign of trouble call 911. Then stay with them until help arrives. Never leave them alone. Absolutely do not throw them into a bed to "sleep it off." While you're with them, keep an eye on their breathing. You can do a few things to make respiration easier, such as rolling them to their side and loosening the clothing around their necks and chest, if they seem to be having trouble.

Don't induce vomiting. People who are severely incapacitated sometimes lose their gag reflex. If you make them throw up something could get caught in their airway and lead to asphyxiation.

SIGNS OF ALCOHOL POISONING

→ They won't wake up
→ Extreme confusion
→ Vomiting while passed out
→ Seizures
→ Slow or irregular breathing—fewer than eight breaths per minute
→ Irregular breathing—10 seconds or more between breaths
→ Abnormal body temperature—either too hot or cold or sweating profusely
→ Abnormal skin color—pale skin or bluish lips

Watch for Potential Sexual Assaults

About half of all sexual assaults involve alcohol use by the survivor.[17] And the perpetrators had been drinking in 79%.[18] In other words, when you throw a party, you've created an environment in which the chance of sexual assault significantly rises. During the party keep an eye out for anything untoward going on. Intervene if you see someone who needs help (for a full discussion of sexual assault and bystander intervention, see chapter 4).

If the Police Show Up

Even if you do absolutely everything right, the police might still knock on your door. Remember, there's a good chance they've come because of a noise complaint. If you're lucky they'll tell you to quiet down—or shut the party down—and be on their way. But things could also get much worse. How you handle yourself during your interaction could be the difference between a warning and a citation.

Hosts Only

This is when the designated hosts need to spring into action. Both should go out to engage the police. One is there to do the talking, the other to act as a witness (arrange who's who in advance). It should only be the two hosts who go outside. You don't want a crowd of onlookers interfering. Go outside, close the door behind you, and walk 20 or so feet away from your house to speak.

Don't Be a Jerk

Think of the police officers as your professor and your interaction with them as a test. Would you ever scrawl a message to your instructor on the top of an exam about how much you hated them? Would you write, "Hey Professor Smith, I just want to let you know I don't like you. And I basically pay your salary, so you really work for me. I bet you got beat up in high school and that's why you became a professor, because you're a sad little man who needs to feel powerful." And if you did do that, would you expect any generosity in your grade?

When talking to an officer of the law, be nice. Shake their hands, introduce yourself, and ask "How can I help you?" They're probably there because you're too loud. Chances are they're not looking to give you a hard time. And even if they are, a bad attitude is only going to make your situation worse.

Don't Get Physical

The police may come into your house—even over your objections (see *State v. Namay*). If they do, just step back. If you try to block them, you could be charged with assault or interfering with an officer. Even if they aren't trying to get into your house, be aware of yourself physically. Give them a warning if you're going to reach into your pockets. Say, "My wallet is in my inside chest jacket pocket; is it okay if I get it out?"

Do what you need to communicate loudly and clearly that you're not a threat and that you're cooperating. The police officers will appreciate it. That will be reflected in how they treat you.

AFTER THE PARTY

De-Litter Your Lawn

Make sure the public-facing parts of your property are presentable. I know, cleaning is that last thing you want to do the morning after a party. You don't have to make everything immaculate. You just need to get what's visible from the street to passable level. A half hour of tidying up will pay all sorts of dividends. A lawn strewn with post-party detritus will draw the wrong kind of attention from both the authorities and your neighbors.

Check In with the Neighbors

Touch base with your neighbors within a day or two of the party. They might have been at their wit's end because of the racket you made. If so, you'll want to know so you can change things up next time around.

Legal Clean Up

Minor offenses, like citations for open containers or excessive noise, usually aren't worth fighting in court. They shouldn't leave a mark on your record. If you made it through the weekend with nothing more than a summary offense, thank whatever god or gods you pray to, pay your fine, and move on.

If you're facing a more serious charge like the possession of alcohol, serving to minors, or public indecency you'll need to find a lawyer. Specifically, you'll need a local attorney who deals with those kinds of cases. Every town has someone who specializes in DUIs, underage drinking, and similar offenses. How do you find this person?

Good attorneys often don't advertise. They don't need to. They get all the work they can handle from referrals. Often the best way to find a competent lawyer is to ask around. Even if you go to school far from home, you're a part of the college community. Connections abound. Talk to a staff member you trust and ask if they have a recommendation. It might be an awkward conversation to start, "Hey Professor Jones, you seem like you should be in jail, you must have an awesome lawyer …?" But it should work. I guarantee you're never more than a few conversations away from finding excellent representation.

CHAPTER SUMMARY

Safety should be your number-one concern when you host a party. Once someone drinks alcohol under your roof it's your duty to ensure they get home, and through the night, safely. Beyond that, hosts need to take steps to ensure their actions, and the acts of others, don't land them in legal trouble.

Noise is what usually draws the authorities to a party. Tell your neighbors that you're having people over beforehand. Ask them to call you, not the police, if things get too loud. Also do a sound check before the party starts. Never post public invitations to a party, physically or online. Invite people privately and ask them not to share the invitation.

It's illegal in every state in the nation to sell alcohol without a liquor license. It's also illegal to furnish alcohol to a minor in every jurisdiction. Every minor you serve could be charged as a separate offense. A party with 17 underage guests could result in 17 citations for serving minors.

The Fourth Amendment right to be free of unreasonable searches doesn't do much to protect college students when they throw parties. On-campus searches are usually performed by RAs or other staff. The Fourth doesn't apply to those employees, even at public schools. Off campus, by the time the police arrive at a party they probably have a right to come in and perform a search.

Social hosts can be held legally liable if one of their guests consumes alcohol, then leaves and harms themselves or someone else. The death of Brandon Narleski and the subsequent civil lawsuit shows how the concept of social host liability has expanded in the recent past.

The best way to keep everyone safe and avoid legal trouble is to assign designated hosts who will stay sober and watch for potential crimes and problems during the party. If the police do arrive, the sober hosts should be the ones who respectfully engage with them.

After the party, it's important to touch base with your neighbors, clean up the public parts of your home, and find a competent attorney if needed.

NOTES

1   College Station Texas Code of Ordinances, Subpart A, General Ordinances, Chapter 26, Miscellaneous Provisions and Offenses, § 26.8.

2   Municipal Code City of Beloit, WI. Chapter 15—Public Peace and Good Order, § 15.12.

3   47 Pa. Stat. § 4-491 (2016).

4   TN Code § 39-17-702 (2021).

5   NM Stat § 60-7B-1 (2021).

6   NM Stat § 31-18-15 (2021).

7   SC Code § 61-4-90 (2021).

8   U.S. Constitution, Amendment IV.

9   "2021-2022 Community Living Guide: Room Entry, Inspection, & Maintenance," University of Nebraska-Lincoln, 10 February 2022, p. 17, https://housing.unl.edu/reslife/pdf/Housing_Community_Living_Guide_2021-22.pdf.

10   State v. Namay, 106 Ohio Misc. 2d 72, 74 (2000).

11   Ibid., 74.

12   Ibid., 72, 75.

13   Ibid., 72, 78.

14   Estate of Narleski v. Gomes, 2020 N.J. LEXIS 993 (2020).

15   Loyer, Susan. "Mom Remembers Son at Sayreville Man's Sentencing." *My Central Jersey*, 13 November 2015, https://www.mycentral-jersey.com/story/news/local/middlesex-county/2015/11/13/sayreville-man-sentenced-fatal-drunk-driving-crash/75723472/.

16   Estate of Narleski v. Gomes.

17   Abbey, Antonia, et al. "Alcohol's Role in Sexual Assault." *Drug and Alcohol Abuse Reviews*, vol. 5, edited by R. R. Watson. Humana Press, 1994, pp. 97–123.

18   Crowell, Nancy A., and Ann W. Burgess. *Understanding Violence against Women*. National Academy Press, 1996.

9 HAZING

TIMOTHY PIAZZA AT PENN STATE

Just after 9:00 p.m. on February 2, 2017, the new members of Penn State's Beta Theta Pi chapter arrived at their house for the first night of initiation. Among them was a 19-year-old freshman from New Jersey named Tim Piazza. He was excited about what was to come. He texted his girlfriend, "They're going to get me fucked up," just before he left for the night.[1]

The new members gathered in the house's great hall but were immediately led in a line, right hand on the shoulder of the man in front, to the living room. They were given a handle of vodka and told they had to, collectively, finish it. After that each new member had to run "the gauntlet"—an obstacle course of sorts with a series of stations. At each stop there was alcohol they had to down. At the first station was a shot of vodka. Next, a run down a hallway where, at the end, each initiate had to shotgun a beer. After that they were forced to guzzle wine from a bag while Beta brothers poured beer on their faces. Finally, each recruit had to make a beer pong shot—for every miss they had to take a drink.[2]

Piazza went through around 9:20 p.m. Including the vodka before the gauntlet, he consumed 18 drinks in the span of 82 minutes.[3] By half past 10:00 he was visibly intoxicated and needed help to stand and walk. At that point, two of the Beta brothers managed to get Piazza, already verging on unconsciousness, to a couch in the great hall.[4]

Security cameras captured most of Piazza's movements that night. At 10:45 Piazza, left unattended, managed to stand up and stagger off. He eventually fell 15 feet down the basement stairs. Some of the Betas carried him back to the great hall a few minutes later. By this point his body was limp and he had a visible, dark bruise emerging on his stomach. After getting him back on the couch one of the other partygoers administered a sternal rub—a test used by EMTs to measure response to pain—to Piazza. He was unresponsive. Another poured alcohol on his face. Again, no response. For the next half hour a few of the Betas kept watch over Piazza and tried to keep him still, first by putting a weighted backpack on him, then by sitting on his legs.[5]

At a quarter past 11:00 sophomore Kordel Davis came into the room. Seeing Piazza's condition he screamed at the others, telling them they needed to get Piazza to the hospital. In response, one of the other Betas slammed Davis up against a wall and told him everything was under control. The recruitment chairman showed up a few minutes later and slapped Piazza three times in the face in an attempt to rouse him. It didn't have any effect.[6]

By 1:00 am, again left unattended, Piazza was vomiting, twitching, and drifting in and out of consciousness. At 5:00 am, he managed to stand up and stagger away from the couch toward the lobby of the house. He fell again, hitting his head on a metal railing as he went down. He tried to get up, but fell again, this time headfirst into a door. Piazza stayed there, passed out, for the next two hours while multiple Betas either walked by him or stepped over his unconscious body.[7]

Around 7:00 a.m. Piazza managed to stand up a final time and, again, staggered off. He fell down the basement steps a second time. Three hours later some of the members found him downstairs, passed out behind a bar. His soon-to-be brothers spent 45 minutes cleaning him up and changing his clothes in an apparent effort to cover their tracks before getting him help. Finally, just before 11:00 a.m. one of them called 911. By this time Piazza's spleen was lacerated, his abdomen was filled with blood, and he had multiple traumatic brain injuries.[8] Fifteen hours later he was pronounced dead.[9]

Twenty-six Penn State Betas were criminally indicted for his death. But the most serious charges were all dropped. Only three members received jail time for their involvement—all less than a year.[10] After the dust settled, legislators in Pennsylvania[11] and New Jersey,[12] Piazza's home state, passed new, stricter anti-hazing laws bearing his name. The university, of course, permanently revoked Beta Theta Pi's chapter and tightened the rules that govern the Greek system. But experts don't think those the reforms went far enough, and fear that, ultimately, they won't make any real difference.[13]

   The Beta Theta Pi house at Penn State.

Piazza's story isn't unique. A college student has died from hazing every year for the last 60 years. The only exception: 2020 when everyone was locked down due to COVID.[14] There were 50 hazing deaths in the U.S. between 2007 and 2017 alone.[15] There were 5 in 2021.[16]

I have to admit, I don't understand any part of hazing. For starters, the responses from administrations and state legislators are always the same. And they don't work. I don't blame either necessarily. Laws and rules are the only tools they have. They're doing what they can.

But this is a culture problem. It won't be solved by regulations that only come into play after a horrific incident. Change has to come from within. That puts the responsibility, and the burden, on you the students. And this is where I get confused—and angry. I can't comprehend how anyone could treat their friends with the abject cruelty and neglect exhibited by the Penn State Betas.

These are Beta Theta Pi's five core values:

- → Mutual Assistance: Betas believe that men are mutually obligated to help others in the honorable labors and aspirations of life.
- → Intellectual Growth: Betas are devoted to continually cultivating their minds, including high standards of academic achievement.
- → Trust: Betas develop absolute faith and confidence in one another by being true to themselves and others.
- → Responsible Conduct: Betas choose to act responsibly, weighing the consequences of their actions on themselves and those around them.

→ Integrity: Betas preserve their character by doing what is morally right and demanding the same from their brothers.[17]

Read through those tenets. Then think about Timothy Piazza's soon-to-be brothers stepping over his unconscious body in the early hours of February 3, 2017. Was that "responsible conduct"? Did they "preserve their character by doing what is morally right"? Did they offer "mutual assistance"? The contrasts between the ideals espoused in the five core values and the actions of the Penn State Betas are hard to reconcile.

I don't mean to be unfairly targeting Beta Theta Pi. Hazing is a serious problem across Greek letter organizations. Seven out of 10 fraternity and sorority members are hazed. And Greeks aren't the worst offenders. Varsity athletes report hazing at slightly higher levels—nearly three quarters said they'd been hazed in the same survey. As did more than half (56%) of the members of college performing arts organizations (e.g., marching bands), 50% of service fraternity and sorority members, 49% of intramural team members, 28% percent of academic club members, and 20% of honor society members.[18] Read that last entry again—20% of honor society members. Unbelievable.

At this point hazing is endemic. And most college students think it's here to stay. In a 2017 survey, 52% of undergrads said that they thought hazing would always be a part of college life.[19] These data points all lead to a simple conclusion: It's critical that college students know how to protect themselves from getting hurt this way.

DEFINING HAZING

There are three components to hazing.

Membership

The activity must be a requirement for joining, or staying in, a group. Most of us associate hazing with the initiation period. But activities at any time during membership could qualify. For example, if all the varsity members of a team are forced to streak through campus before the season starts, that's hazing even for the veterans who've been on the team for years and are presumably streaking for their second or third time.

Abuse

If an activity humiliates or degrades, or if it has the potential to cause harm—either physical or emotional—then it's hazing. How will you know if something seemingly benign has crossed the line into abuse? As with most things, trust your gut—especially if you're on the receiving end. If what's being asked of you makes you feel vulnerable or embarrassed or puts you in danger it's probably hazing. If you're on the organizing side of the equation, a good rule of thumb is if you wouldn't feel comfortable telling your grandmother about an activity, there's a good chance it's hazing.

Most of the hazing incidents that make the news involve alcohol. Participating in drinking games is the most reported hazing behavior, at 53%.[20] But alcohol isn't a necessary component. Anything that degrades or harms qualifies. Having to wear embarrassing clothes, not being able to associate with certain people, sleep deprivation or being woken at all hours of the night, even being forced to sing or chant, could qualify as hazing under the right circumstances.

Lack of Choice

Most school policies state that an activity can be hazing even if the target agreed to participate. This makes sense. The line between voluntary and mandatory is hard to delineate when peer pressure and uneven power dynamics are involved. Even if you don't explicitly force someone to do something, they might still see it as mandatory. And, even if a new member knows participation isn't strictly required, they might think that opting out will result in repercussions—like rejection or taunting. The safest approach, then, is to assume that anything you ask newcomers to do will be interpreted by them as a nonnegotiable demand.

Most Hazing Isn't Headline Worthy

It's important to remember that the extreme kind of hazing, like the incident at Penn State, represents only a tiny portion of infractions. Most hazing is low key. Seemingly benign things could be forms of hazing. Again, if a task is directed at newcomers and it's used to humiliate, it's hazing. Take, for example, learning an official oath or having to memorize facts about the history of an organization. Both are reasonable. But if full members are allowed to quiz initiates on the spot and can punish them if they get something wrong, that crosses the line. Likewise with chores: Certainly, every member of a fraternity should be expected to pitch in and maintain the house. But treating younger members as servants goes too far. Context matters.

A recent court case about mandatory study time illustrates this well. The Sigma Lambda Upsilon chapter at the University of Virginia required all new members to spend 25 hours a week hitting the books, which was extremely taxing. When the university found out about it, they suspended the chapter for violating the school's hazing policy, which prohibited activities "designed to produce ... mental or physical harassment, humiliation, fatigue, degradation, ridicule, shock, or injury." The sorority sued, arguing the suspension violated their First Amendment rights of association and their civil rights. The court held that the school was well within its authority to regulate the sorority's behavior.[21]

Again, think of context. Wanting your sisters to get good grades is a laudable goal. But there's a huge difference between a group's leadership encouraging academic excellence by setting up informal, voluntary study groups and requiring new members to study at a specific place and time for hours on end. The former is altruistic. The latter is hazing.

School Policies

As I've said many times elsewhere in this book, the school's code of conduct is the most important set of rules for any college student. Find the hazing policy in your student handbook, if there is one, and read through it. It'll probably contain the three elements in some way, shape or form. Here's Auburn's definition of hazing:

A. Auburn University defines hazing as any group or individual conduct, action or activity, regardless of location of incident or consent of participants, that by design, negligence, or recklessness:

1. Occurs in the context of initiation, admission into, affiliation with, or as a condition of continued membership in a group or organization and;

2. Inflicts or intends to inflict physical or mental harm, excessive fatigue, or distress or which may demean, disgrace, humiliate or degrade a reasonable person;

3. Presents a threat to a student's health or safety, including but not limited to any brutality of a

>   physical nature, or physical activity that could
>   adversely affect the physical and/or mental health
>   or safety of a student;
>
> 4. Unreasonably interferes with a student's ability to
>   succeed in an academic environment; such activities
>   would include but are not limited to creating
>   excessive fatigue and not allowing reasonable
>   preparation time for academic pursuits.[22]

This is a well-written definition. It hits all the main points in an understandable way. Notice how it deals with lack of choice. The first sentence says an activity could be hazing regardless of the "consent of the participants." Then it states under heading 1 that hazing occurs in "the context of initiation, admission into, affiliation with, or as a condition of continued membership in a group or organization." That combination covers the assent issue well.

Parts 2, 3, and 4 do a good job of describing the abusive nature of hazing. Part 1 covers mental and physical harm, including humiliation. Part 2 covers the fact that risky behaviors that could harm someone, even if they ultimately don't result in an injury, also qualify as hazing. And 4 states anything that interferes with a student's ability to succeed academically, like sleep deprivation, would qualify. Finally, part 5, which isn't included in the excerpt, states that inducing students to violate any law or policy constitutes hazing.

State Laws

It's important to be aware of your state's statute. At the time of writing, 44 states and the District of Columbia had hazing laws in place. The exceptions are Alaska, Hawaii, Montana, New Mexico, South Dakota, and Wyoming. Here's New Jersey's law. It's one of the strictest and most comprehensive in the country. You'll notice it looks a lot like the Auburn policy in how it defines a violation:

> 1. a. A person is guilty of hazing, if, in connection with
>   initiation of applicants to or members of a student
>   or fraternal organization, whose membership is pri-
>   marily students or alumni of the organization or an
>   institution of higher education, the person knowingly
>   or recklessly:
>
>   (1) causes, coerces, or otherwise induces another
>   person to commit an act that violates federal or
>   State criminal law;

(2) causes, coerces, or otherwise induces another person to consume any food, liquid, alcoholic liquid, drug or other substance which subjects the person to a risk of emotional or physical harm or is otherwise deleterious to the person's health;

(3) subjects another person to abuse, mistreatment, harassment, or degradation of a physical nature, including, but not limited to, whipping, beating, branding, excessive calisthenics, or exposure to the elements;

(4) subjects another person to abuse, mistreatment, harassment, or degradation of a mental or emotional nature, including, but not limited to, activity adversely affecting the mental or emotional health or dignity of the individual, sleep deprivation, exclusion from social contact, or conduct that could result in extreme embarrassment;

(5) subjects another person to abuse, mistreatment, harassment, or degradation of a sexual nature; or

(6) subjects another person to any other activity that creates a reasonable likelihood of bodily injury to the person.[23]

If the hazing results in death or serious injury, it's a third-degree crime, which carries a three- to five-year prison sentence and up to a $15,000 fine. Hazing without injury is treated as a "disorderly person" offense, which carries a maximum sentence of 6 months jail time and a fine of up to $1,000. Plus, the statute adds fines on top of the standard sentence—a $1,000 to $5,000 additional penalty for a first offense and $5,000 to $15,000 for second and subsequent offenses.[24]

On the other end of the severity spectrum is Kansas's law which states the following:

(a) Hazing is recklessly coercing, demanding or encouraging another person to perform, as a condition of membership in a social or fraternal organization, any act which could reasonably be expected to result in great bodily harm, disfigurement or death or which is done in a manner whereby great bodily harm, disfigurement or death could be inflicted.

(b) Hazing is a class B nonperson misdemeanor.[25]

This definition is incredibly lax. It only applies to "social or fraternal" organizations. And it only covers acts that could lead to death, disfigurement, or bodily harm. The penalties are also minor. A class B nonperson misdemeanor in Kansas results in, at most, a six-month prison sentence and a $1,000 fine.[26]

Find your state's statute. It's important that you understand it. Then pray it never comes into play at your organization. State laws are rarely invoked unless there's been a death or serious injury. Even in states like New Jersey, that delineate penalties for activities that harm egos and psyches, law enforcement rarely gets involved when there's been no physical harm.

PREVENTING HAZING

For Student Leaders

Know the Rules (and Make Your Own)

If you're an upper-level student and a member of any kind of campus organization, it's your responsibility to understand your school's policy and the applicable state laws concerning hazing. Members of Greek letter organizations, of course, know that they have to keep an eye on this issue. But hazing happens across all types of clubs and teams. If it's your second year in the marching band, your third season on the varsity squad, or you're one of only a few seniors on the student activities committee, get familiar with the rules.

Do this even if you don't have an official leadership role. As an older student you have implicit power. Even if you're never actually in charge of less-senior students, you'll still be able to keep an eye on your peers' actions and check them if they cross the line.

Also consider enacting an anti-hazing policy specific to your group. Outline what's acceptable and what's not. Again, do this no matter what kind of club you belong to. Never had a hazing problem on your quidditch team? Great. Keep it that way by codifying the civility. It can't hurt. And if things do take a turn for the worse, you'll have some bright line rules to stand on when you're trying to put things right.

Change the Power Dynamic and Communicate

Do anything you can to break down the barriers between leadership and initiates. Involve new members in as much of the organizational decision-making process as you can. Set aside specific times for the youngest members of your organization to discuss their experiences without the fear of retribution. Have that kind of meeting regularly. You might be inadvertently wearing newcomers down without even knowing it, so give them ample chances to speak up.

On the flip side, try to avoid activities in which more senior members can exert power over their younger counterparts. Very few of us have an innate desire to haze our "inferiors," but when people are given more power than they can handle, errors are made.

Plan Ahead

Along the same lines, avoid situations in which the organization's leadership has to make decisions on the fly. Mistakes are more likely to happen under pressure. Plan activities as far ahead as possible. Have concise schedules and parameters. Make sure that all the senior members of your group understand their roles.

Capitalize on Campus Resources

Your group doesn't exist in a vacuum. Talk with other organizations on campus to see what strategies and programs have worked well for them. Also ask them about their failures. Learning about others' mistakes can be just as, if not more, instructive than hearing about their successes.

And don't forget that the school itself has ample resources. If you're having trouble with anything, even understanding how your school's policy works, reach out to the dean of students office. I guarantee they'll be thrilled you're asking questions and trying to avoid a problem in the first place rather than trying to put the hazing fire out afterward.

For New Members

New members often think they're powerless. The truth is that you have more control over your destiny than you realize. Even if it's your first year, or your first day, in a club or on a team, you're vital. Without fresh blood organizations cease to exist. Use that power to stand up for yourself and your fellow newcomers.

Talk

Share what you're going through with others, even if you've been sworn to secrecy about the initiation process. In fact, share what you're going through especially if you've been sworn to secrecy. Demanding confidentiality is a red flag. It often denotes abuse. Communicate with people you trust about your experiences, your feelings, and the effects any activities are having on you. A neutral perspective can be invaluable.

Connect

Make sure you stay connected with your friends and peers who aren't part of the organization. Groups that haze often use isolation as a tactic to keep their members from questioning what they're going through. Take the time to meet with your other friends. Your life will probably be hectic. You'll need to make a real effort. Schedule dinners or coffee with your support group. Also, most campuses offer confidential counseling services. If you don't feel comfortable talking to your classmates, make an appointment with a mental health provider.

Unite, Refuse, and Report

Talk with the other initiates about the process. If you don't like what's happening, refuse to participate. Critical mass equals undeniable power. If a significant portion of the class puts their feet down and says "We're not putting up with this," things will change, fast. The leadership needs you just as much, if not more, than you need them. Think about it, if half, or even a third, of a fraternity's new members drop out, that puts a tremendous amount of pressure on the house— financially and otherwise. It's the same with any other team or club. Without new participants, groups cease to exist.

However things play out, tell the school authorities about the hazing. That might feel disloyal. But if the more senior members of your group are hazing you, have they actually earned your loyalty? And if you really do care about a group, reporting infractions and starting a reform process will result in a stronger, and longer-lasting, organization.

Protect

Finally, if there's an immediate threat to your or someone else's safety, forget everything else and intervene. Don't analyze the situation. Don't worry about potential punishments. Just act.

CHAPTER SUMMARY

On the evening of February 2, 2017, Tim Piazza, a new member of the Beta Theta Pi fraternity at Penn State, consumed 18 alcoholic beverages in 82 minutes as part of an initiation ritual. Over the course of the night, in his drunken state, Piazza fell multiple times and suffered a lacerated spleen and traumatic brain injuries. It was obvious that Piazza needed medical attention, but his soon-to-be brothers ignored his injuries for the entire night. They finally called an ambulance the next morning. But it was too late. Piazza died of his injuries in the early morning hours of February 4th.

Piazza's story is horrific, but not unique. At least one college student has died from hazing every year for the last 60 years (except for 2020 when colleges were shut down). There were 50 hazing deaths in the U.S. between 2007 and 2017 alone. Hazing isn't confined to fraternities. It's a problem across all types of campus clubs and sports. Varsity athletes actually haze more than Greek letter organizations. It's also prevalent in performing arts groups, such as marching bands, intramural teams, service organizations, and even honor societies.

There are three components to hazing. First, the activity must be part of the process to join or stay in a group. Second, it must be abusive in some way; it must humiliate or have the potential to cause harm. Finally, there must be a lack of choice to participate. The last part is the trickiest. It's difficult for there to be true consent given the power dynamics and peer pressure at play. Full members of the group should assume that all initiates perceive requests as demands.

Hazing incidents that involve obscene amounts of alcohol or intense physical abuse grab headlines. But most hazing is much more subtle. Any task that's directed toward newcomers that's used to humiliate is hazing. Having to recite an oath or sing a song on demand, performing household chores, having to wear embarrassing clothing, and even mandatory study groups could be hazing. Context matters.

Most states have laws that prohibit hazing, but they're generally only enforced after the fact. Many schools have anti-hazing policies as well. But hazing is a culture problem. Preventing hazing is the responsibility of students. Established members of groups can prevent hazing by communicating with their initiates, diminishing the power differential between full and members, and carefully planning events. New members can also prevent hazing. By uniting and refusing to participate, they can change the organizational culture.

NOTES

1   Flanagan, Caitlin. "Death at a Penn State Fraternity." *The Atlantic*, 15 November 2017, https://www.theatlantic.com/magazine/archive/2017/11/a-death-at-penn-state/540657/.

2   Alexandersen, Christian. "They Call It 'The Gauntlet': What a Penn State Student Drank at Frat Party." *Penn Live*, 5 May 2017, https://www.pennlive.com/news/2017/05/they_call_it_the_gauntlet_what.html.

3   Vendel, Christine. "What Does 18 Drinks in 82 Minutes Look Like? Penn State Hazing Death Timeline." *Penn Live*, 15 November 2017, https://www.pennlive.com/news/2017/11/penn_state_hazing_death_18_dri.html.

4   Vasile, Sarah. "Timeline: The Events from the Night Leading Up to and Surrounding the Death of Timothy Piazza." *Daily Collegian*, 5 May 2017, https://www.collegian.psu.edu/news/crime_courts/timeline-the-events-from-the-night-leading-up-to-and-surrounding-the-death-of-timothy/article_b0cd4594-31d3-11e7-ab7e-1f8d2b2a1f24.html.

5   Ibid.

6   Ibid.

7   Ibid.

8   Flanagan, "Death at a Penn State Fraternity."

9   Vasile, "Timeline."

10   Holcombe, Madeline. "3 Fraternity Brothers Sentenced to Jail in Penn State Hazing Death." *CNN*, 3 April 2019, https://www.cnn.com/2019/04/03/us/tim-piazza-fraternity-member-hazing-sentences/index.html.

11   Thompson, Madeleine, and Sarah Ganim. "Pennsylvania Governor Signs Anti-Hazing Bill Named for Deceased Penn State Student." *CNN*, 8 December 2018, https://www.cnn.com/2018/10/19/us/tim-piazza-anti-hazing-bill/index.html.

12   Baldwin, Carley. "Tim Piazza's Law Makes NJ Strictest State in the Nation on Hazing." *Patch*, 3 September 2021, https://patch.com/new-jersey/woodbridge/tim-piazzas-law-makes-nj-strictest-state-nation-hazing.

13   Ortiz, Erik. "Do Penn State's Reforms after Hazing death of Timothy Piazza Go Far Enough?" *CNN*, 2 June 2017, https://www.nbcnews.com/storyline/hazing-in-america/do-penn-state-s-reforms-after-hazing-death-timothy-piazza-n767746.

14   Kennedy, Peyton. "2020 Was First Year in 60 with No Hazing-Related Deaths; 2021 Has Not Started as Bright." *WTAJ*, 2 March 2021, https://www.wtaj.com/news/2020-first-year-in-60-with-no-hazing-related-deaths-2021-has-not-started-as-bright/.

15   Nuwer, Hank. "Unofficial Hazing Clearing House." *U.S. Hazing Deaths Database Part 2: 2000–2022*, 2022, https://www.hanknuwer.com/hazing-destroying-young-lives/ Accessed 6 November 2022.

16   Ibid.

17   Beta Theta Pi. *44th edition of the Code of Regulations of Beta Theta Pi*. Betha Theta Pi, 2022, https://www.beta.org/wp-content/uploads/2022/08/Code-of-Beta-Theta-Pi_44th-Edition_08.12.2022.pdf.

18   Allan, Elizabeth J., and Mary Madden. "Hazing in View: College Students at Risk: Initial Findings from the National Study of Student Hazing." *Hazing Research and Prevention, Auburn University*, 11 March 2008, https://ocm.auburn.edu/stop_hazing/National_Hazing_Study.pdf.

19   Abdul-Alim, Jamaal. "College Students: Hazing Here to Stay." *Diverse Issues in Higher Education*, 18 September 2017, https://www.diverseeducation.com/students/article/15101280/college-students-hazing-here-to-stay.

20   Allan and Madden, "Hazing in View."

21   Sigma Lambda Upsilon v. University of Virginia 503 F.Supp 3d 433 (2020).

22   "Anti-Hazing Policy." *Auburn University*, 2022, https://sites.auburn.edu/admin/universitypolicies/Policies/AntiHazingPolicy.pdf.

23   NJ Rev Stat § 2C:40-3 (2021).

24   NJ Rev Stat § 2C:40-3 (2021).

25   KS Stat § 21-5418 (2021).

26   KS Stat § 21-6810 (2021).

Credit

Fig. 9.1: Source: https://www.cbsnews.com/news/penn-state-fraternity-beta-theta-pi-criticized-renting-rooms-timothy-piazza-death/.

Index

About the Author

C.L. Lindsay III is one of the nation's leading experts in student discipline and higher education law. He has spent the last 20 years working with college students, teaching them about their legal rights and responsibilities. He has given more than 1,500 invited lectures at colleges and universities, high schools, and military bases across the country. He is one of the most popular lecturers on the college circuit today.

For eight years he wrote a nationally distributed syndicated write-in column discussing college students' legal issues for Knight Ridder's college wire service. He has also taught courses in law and literature at the University of Pennsylvania. He has been cited as an expert on student rights in numerous national and regional publications including *The Chronicle of Higher Education, The Chicago Tribune, Newsweek*, and *The Christian Science Monitor.* His radio and television appearances include CBS News Radio, MSNBC Live, and NPR's Radio Times with Marty Moss-Coane.

His first book, *The College Student's Guide to the Law: Get a Grade Changed, Keep Your Stuff Private, Throw a Police-Free Party, and More!* was published in 2005 by Rowman and Littlefield. He graduated from Denison University in 1993 and received a law degree from the University of Michigan in 1996.